MONEY IN THE COOKIE JAR

MONEY IN THE COOKIE JAR

The Christian Homemaker's Guide to Making Money at Home

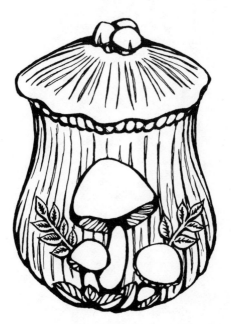

Edith Flowers Kilgo

BAKER BOOK HOUSE
Grand Rapids, Michigan

First printing, March 1980
Second printing, September 1980
Third printing, February 1981

Contents

Introduction

Today's woman has choices. Unlike her grandmother, she does not *have* to be a full-time homemaker. However, in spite of the difficulties in trying to raise a family on Dad's paycheck alone, she may *choose* a full-time homemaking career rather than a career outside her home. The Christian mother, in particular, finds pleasure in giving her children her full-time companionship and guidance. She is willing to learn new recipes for beans and hamburger and to wear last year's dresses in exchange for the privilege of staying home and raising her family in accordance with her Christian principles.

Unfortunately, today's economic situation may force the Christian mother to reluctantly take a job outside her home. Then she may find herself growing discouraged or even resentful. She's caught in a seemingly impossible dilemma. If she does go out to work, she feels guilty and accuses herself of neglecting her family. Yet, if she gives up her paying job, she feels even more guilty about seeing her husband work two jobs to supply the family's needs.

But there is a workable solution to the homemaker's problem. Thousands of women have solved their financial and emotional problems by finding ways to make money without leaving home.

Although endless possibilities for home businesses exist, the Christian woman has much more to consider than just the variety of ways money can be made. In addition, she wants time for church and family activities and time for her civic responsibilities. She also wants a clean house, nutritious meals, and a satisfied family. The continued good will of her neighbors is important to her, too, so she wants a home business that that will be in the best interests of her neighborhood. Recognizing her Christian responsibility to obey the law, she carefully takes care of legal matters such as business licenses, taxes, and social security payments. Making money is important to her, but not as important as maintaining her Christian testimony in every aspect of her life.

Finding You

WHY START A HOME BUSINESS?

Money, money, money—everybody talks about it, most of us think about it, and we who are Christians try not to love it. Yet, in spite of our good intentions, there inevitably comes a time when we need more of it.

For those of us who are full-time wives and mothers, either by choice or by necessity, there eventually comes a time when we really wish for just a few dollars to call our own. Maybe it comes at a time when our husband's birthday is near and we are faced with the choice of paying for his present with money he has earned or putting the gift on a charge account for him to reckon with later. Either way leaves us with the thought that a gift paid for with "his" money isn't really a gift at all.

Sometimes that siren call of filthy lucre comes on a giddy spring day when, in spite of a size fourteen body, a woman feels like an adolescent and longs for a bottle of lilac-scented bath salts, even though yielding to that temptation would sentence the family to a meatless diet for the rest of the week.

1

As stay-at-home wives and mothers, we really do try to content ourselves as we sew up the rips in last season's coat. Resolutely we mend and darn to the heady odor of bubbling hamburger casserole.

"I really do want to be a full-time wife and mother," we moan in unison, "and I'm sure that's the Lord's will for my life, but wouldn't it be nice to have a few extra dollars, too? Is it wrong for me to be thinking about making money?"

No, it's not! There's absolutely no harm in making money with a home business, as long as the business does not take precedence over your commitment to God and to your family.

GOD'S STAMP OF APPROVAL

Proverbs 31 describes a virtuous woman. She is pictured as nearly perfect in the performance of her duties as any homemaker you will ever find. She kept house, sewed, cooked, tended to her civic duties, and made her husband and children proud. She also made time for additional tasks. The virtuous woman was a part-time career woman as well as a full-time homemaker!

Verse 24 says, "She maketh fine linen, and selleth it; and delivereth girdles unto the merchant." The virtuous woman used her spare time profitably. She made handwork and belts as a means of bringing in a little extra money for her family. When we take a closer look at her circumstances, we wonder why this was necessary. Her family must have been wealthier than middle-class.

Verse 15 indicates her position was such that she had household servants: "She raiseth also while it is yet night, and giveth meat to her household, and a portion to her maidens." Verse 20 tells us she ministered to the poor, and this is an indication that she had the necessary funds for engaging in benevolence: "She stretcheth out her hand to the poor; yea, she reacheth forth her hands to the needy." Verses 21 and 22 also mention other signs of wealth: "She is not afraid of the snow for her household; for all her household are clothed with scarlet. She maketh herself coverings of tapestry; her clothing is silk and purple." Verse 23 says her husband was a well respected politician: "Her husband is known in the gates, when he sitteth among the elders of the land."

Why would a woman with wealth, influence, and position bother with running a home business? Perhaps, in addition to the pleasure of making extra money, the virtuous woman found personal satisfaction and fulfillment in what she did. Her home business was possibly a creative outlet for her.

PUTTING FIRST THINGS FIRST

Of all her many commendable attributes, the most significant characteristic of the virtuous woman is found in verse 15: "She riseth also while it is yet night, and giveth meat to her household, and a portion to her maidens." Getting out of bed before daybreak involved sacrifice, but the virtuous woman gladly prepared a nutritious breakfast for her family even though she could have easily delegated that task to some of her household staff. Perhaps she arose in darkness for a reason even more important than preparing her family's breakfast. Early morning, before the rest of the family gets out of bed, is, for many homemakers, the only solitary and quiet portion of the day. What better opportunity could there be for having a quiet time alone with the Lord? A few minutes spent in Bible reading and prayer gives any homemaker the vital strength she needs for coping with the remainder of the day. Think about this aspect of your life as you, too, begin planning to start a home business. Remember that any work which takes you away from your accustomed time of communion with the Lord is not going to be successful.

The virtuous woman of Proverbs 31 is a model after which Christian women can seek to pattern themselves. Since she, too, had a part-time job, both for personal satisfaction and for making money, it becomes evident the Lord has no objections to a woman's efforts to make money, provided she puts her relationship with God and with her family ahead of her money-making endeavors.

Guilt does not have to be part of the inventory in a home business if a woman has her priorities in order. After seeking God's guidance and receiving His answer, and after receiving her husband's assurance that he agrees with her plans, a homemaker can confidently begin considering the kind of work she will do.

Of course, the options available for obtaining those few extra dollars range from baby-sitting to giving xylophone lessons—with a thousand possibilities in between. Your route to success lies in the matters of ability and temperament. Sometimes ability can be changed, but temperament is *you*, so before plunging into any kind of business, sit down with yourself and get better acquainted. Decide on priorities, goals, and aptitudes according to your personality. What kind of woman are you?

DEFINING TEMPERAMENT

Are you contented with your role as a full-time wife and mother? Do you awake each morning filled with delight at the prospect of such wonderful activities as teaching your preschooler to finger-paint? Are you excited by compiling recipes for time-consuming yeast breads? Do you hum contentedly while designing and sewing a three piece suit for your husband? If these things are an accurate description of you, then consider yourself as a dyed-in-the-wool, bona fide homemaker.

What is a homemaker? A homemaker is not merely a person with the ability to keep an antiseptically clean house: she also enjoys her house and the family who lives there. For some homemakers, keeping a house clean is not a chore, but an exciting adventure. If you pillow your head at night content in the glow of freshly waxed furniture and are lulled to sleep by the heady aroma of bathroom deodorizer, it is safe to say you are the kind of homemaker who would never be happy as anything else.

Yet many successful homemakers aren't like that at all. They are full-time homemakers because either they, or their husbands, want it that way. Homemaking is their calling, but the mechanics of the job aren't especially thrilling to them.

A clue that you are this type of woman is if you find yourself muttering, "Just sixteen years, four months, and twenty-six days and they will all be through with school and I can sleep late!" If this sounds like you, answer these questions: Do you dust the tops of the furniture and figure the legs aren't noticed much anyway? Is your idea of a home-cooked meal something cooked on the grill and finished off with a bowl of ice cream? If these things describe you, you are likely Cathy Casual and not Sally Spotless. You're totally devoted to your home and family, but no one accuses you of fanaticism.

4

Why must you take such a close look at yourself in this evaluation? If you are serious about making money at home, you need to thoroughly understand and accept your own personality and your own way of life. That's the only way to develop a home business that is totally compatible with *you*. It doesn't matter what someone else on your block is doing successfully; your only consideration is what suits you and your way of doing things.

The home-oriented woman will never be content with a job which detracts from her primary goals of keeping a spotless house, enjoying the company of her children, and exercising her creativity through her cooking and sewing. Any moneymaking effort that infringes on her primary goals will ultimately lead to sleepless nights, ulcers, or crying spells. No amount of money is worth that kind of torture. If you are this kind of woman, accept yourself as you are and don't try to change into Mrs. Executive for the sake of a few extra dollars. Instead, select a home business that utilizes your homemaking skills. Perhaps you would be happy baby-sitting, selling potted plants, marketing your own home-baked bread, or running a home sewing business. In Jeremiah 1:5, Jeremiah was reminded that God had formed him, known him before birth, and chosen a life's work for him. Likewise, the Lord made each of us as we are and has a plan for us to follow. Any kind of business that goes against the personality God created in us, will ultimately fail.

The woman who is staying home because of reasons other than her own personal desire to do so should also assess her situation. Perhaps your reason for being a stay-at-home is because your husband insists that he make the living and you keep the house, or perhaps you had a working mother and don't want your children to be as lonely as you were when you came home to an empty house each day. Whatever your reason, be honest with yourself. If you aren't Henrietta Homemaker, face the fact and accept yourself as you are. Then you won't fall into the trap of trying to make a few extra dollars by doing something you hate. If your own children drive you to tears, then you must realize you are not suited to be a baby-sitter. If sewing on a button is your idea of cruel and unfair punishment, then making stuffed animals for the consignment shop won't bring you happiness, either. The important thing to remember is that God made you into the person you are and gave you other talents to compensate for what you lack in housekeeping skills. Be yourself! Think in terms of home typing jobs, organizational jobs, or even dog walking if the great outdoors appeals to you. *You* decide what fits, but just be sure it isn't a career requiring homemaking aptitude.

Match your lifestyle with potential moneymaking opportunities. Temporarily put aside your educational background—or lack of it—your talents, available work space, amount of spare time, and thoughts of the approaching Christmas season's financial crunch, and focus instead on yourself. For right now, think only about the following questions. Answer them honestly in order to determine your own priorities and interests.

QUESTIONS TO CONSIDER

1. Do I feel that starting a home business meets with God's approval?

2. Does my family approve of my plans?

3. Will this job contribute in any way to my ability to serve the Lord and to keep my family happy?

4. Can I take on a part-time home business without sacrificing my time alone with God or my time with my family?

5. How do I feel about my homemaking duties?

6. Can I be happy with a job that causes me to change my schedule and perhaps give up some of my homemaking duties?

7. Can I do this job without driving myself and my family to either ulcers or the tranquilizer bottle?

8. Can I make money without feeling guilty about giving up my title as a full-time wife and mother?

9. Why do I want to earn money?

10. How much do I need to earn?

What About the Family?

HOW DOES MY HUSBAND FEEL ABOUT A HOME BUSINESS?

After coming to terms with yourself, the next big hurdle is to convince your family that you mean business about going into business. If you've been married as long as a week, you have no doubt noticed that what husbands *say* and what they *think* may at times be as different as Antarctica and the Sahara Desert. The foot-putting-down husband has been more or less replaced by a more puzzling model. This new breed of spouse comes in two varieties in regard to having a wife earn money at home—the "Do what you think is best" model and the "Well, that's great!" variety. However, don't be misled by exterior appearances. Underneath that facade may lie a latent foot-putter-downer. Unfortunately, even if you've lived forty-nine years with the fellow, you sometimes don't know what he *really* wants you to do until it's too late.

Perhaps the safest thing to do is to consider your husband's childhood and possibly glean from his attitude toward his mother how he feels about your staying home to be a full-time homemaker. My husband wants me to stay at home with our daughter because that is what his mother did. I want to stay home with our daughter because I had a working mother. We have the same outlook but we arrived at it in different ways!

If your husband feels strongly about your staying home to care for the children, this will give you a clue that you can obtain harmony at your house only by putting the children's needs first. On the other hand, if he doesn't seem to mind if you occasionally leave the children with a sitter, but he comes unglued if the beds are not made, you can deduce that fear of dirt, disease, and dishes is likely to be his chief objection to your moneymaking efforts.

If your reply is, "What difference does it make what he thinks; I'll do as I please, anyhow!" you had better start hoping that your second and third marriages will work out better than the one you're ruining right now! More than just a home business will fail if a wife has an attitude like that.

THE HOME BUSINESS AND ITS EFFECT ON THE FAMILY

In our family we discuss major decisions as a family unit, but other families successfully follow a less traditional method of reaching decisions. If you and your husband make decisions without consulting the children, a home business requires a different approach. Even if you work only two or three hours a week at your moneymaking endeavor, the results will inevitably affect your family in numerous ways. There is no home job that won't occasionally disrupt your home life, especially if you deal with customers. You can, of course, minimize the disruptions with careful planning and good management, but don't naively assume that no rough spots will occur. No one manages that well. At least if you hold a family conference about the matter you won't be confronted later by a pouty child muttering, "Who told you to start that crummy old job anyway?"

WHAT ABOUT CHILDREN AND A HOME BUSINESS?

No matter how young or old your children are, as long as they live in your home, you cannot run a successful home business without their help. Whether the help is involuntary—such as a three-year-old taking a nap while mommy works—or considerable—such as a teen-ager cheerfully mowing the grass—you *must* have your children's cooperation in order to succeed.

Even Christian parents sometimes feel guilty about making their children do work at home, but the principle is biblical. Proverbs 22:6 says, "Train up a child in the way he should go: and when he is old, he will not depart from it." Part of that training is teaching your children chores necessary for assuming the responsibilities of adulthood. The entire course of Jewish history was changed because a little girl named Miriam capably baby-sat in the manner she was instructed by her mother. Although David grew up to become king of Israel, his parents had trained him in the task of tending sheep. Samuel, who became a great man of God, began serving at the temple soon after his second birthday. Responsibilities offer children a chance to grow spiritually, too.

Although Christians try to raise their children not to over-value the importance of money, quite a bit of competition comes from television, magazines, and friends. For this reason, it helps to discuss your financial situation with your children. Your five-year-old won't be able to comprehend complicated budget problems, but just being consulted on the matter of your home business will make him feel more grown-up and more likely to cooperate. Older children may even be able to offer helpful ideas which you have not yet considered. Even a disinterested teen-ager can readily grasp the economic situation when you point out that unless you can earn some money he will have to wear last year's suit even if the pants are short enough to show three inches of his leg. Then suddenly he'll get interested in helping mother with a home business!

It helps to show your children that they, too, can enjoy benefits of your new job. As my daughter, Karen, grows, I proportionately raise her allowance as she assumes more household responsibilities. I am not paying her for doing her chores, but rather I am letting her have a part in earning the money I make. I could not do my job without her help. She is also old enough now to realize Daddy's income pays our necessary expenses, and Mommy's contribution buys a few extras. Karen is only ten but we discuss finances freely in her presence, and she has a realistic view of employment, income, and budgets.

Unfortunately, many of us have one built-in problem that will inevitably clash head on with any moneymaking venture. We want to make our children's lives easier than our own childhood was. Yet giving children a too soft life actually does them an injustice. Think back to your own childhood. Do you suppose your mom really had cruelty in mind when she insisted you do the dinner dishes? No, not likely. She wanted to teach you a few things—how to become a good housekeeper, how to finish what you start, and how to negotiate labor relations with your brothers and sisters. Did you really suffer so much from her "injustice"? Including your children in household chores will in a similar manner build their characters while alleviating some of your work load.

TRAINING CHILDREN FOR HOUSEHOLD TASKS

If you have decided to enter a home business while your children are small, give yourself a pat on the back for being so clever. Toddlers are highly moldable. Later on, they won't be prone to pose such questions as, "Why do I have to make my bed?" or "Everybody else gets to go, why do I have to do work?" If the children are small, you can approach the chores as a game. A great many jobs we have to do would be more enjoyable if we hadn't learned that work and fun are separate classifications. Therefore, do your toddlers a favor—teach them to find pleasure in the things they have to do.

Although it does take time and patience to train children in household chores, eventually they'll become adept in their duties, and you will have acquired for yourself some free time for your home business.

The real secret of success with small children is to praise their accomplishments—if you can do so honestly. Respect their attempts at being helpful and never re-do their work. If you're convinced they've done their best, let the results stand, even if the work is not perfect. However, if they've intentionally done a poor job, having them re-do the task will convince them that it is quicker to do the work right the first time.

If your children are older and have never done household chores, the first few weeks of the new schedule will be hectic. For this reason, it's a good idea to take a few weeks to train the troops before you plunge too deeply into your home business.

Otherwise, you may feel the need to buy tranquilizers by the case!

It also helps to have children write lists of things to do with notations of approximate times necessary for accomplishing each task. In this way they can challenge their own record and can try to set a new speed record for getting finished.

If you can't agree with them on what does and does not constitute a clean room, try having them draw up a list of specifications. After they put down on paper such items as, "no junk on the floor, no stuff under the bed, and no chewed gum on the desk," they'll begin to understand what is expected of them.

Sometimes a less traditional approach to the work load might be beneficial. Try experimenting with different jobs to add to the enthusiasm. Perhaps your teen-age son would prefer to cook dinner while his teen-age sister washes the car. Who knows—you might get fewer squabbles that way. Besides, what really matters is getting the job done.

HUSBANDS AND HOUSEWORK

Most husbands really do think it's fine for their wives to make a few extra dollars while they enrich their lives, enjoy new activities, and make new friends. However, when it comes to sharing household chores some husbands say: "Housework? That's your job. If you can't handle housework and a business maybe you should give up the business."

The problem is that most women don't begin a home career until after they have been full-time wives and mothers for a number of years. By then husbands and children have settled into a comfortable routine. After talking with numerous women who have jobs at home, I've made the following discoveries: Nine out of ten husbands promise to help with the housework when their wives begin a moneymaking venture at home, but ten out of ten husbands don't help. Of course there's always a possibility that your may be different—just as there's a possibility that the government may abolish taxes!

About the only exceptions I've found are among very young couples, very elderly retired couples, or couples who both participate in the home business venture. If both of you spend Saturdays making quilted batik or tooled leather, then maybe both of you can spend Friday evening waxing floors together.

I'm not suggesting that your husband won't cooperate with your home business, I'm saying that his idea of helping may not be the same as yours. *You* think helping means that he'll vacuum for you occasionally. *He* thinks helping means saying, "Aw, don't worry about things so much. Vacuuming once a week ought to be enough." *You* think helping means he'll pick up his clothes. *He* thinks helping means seeing that the children pick up theirs.

You'll spare yourself a lot of grief if, regardless of how successful your business becomes, you always remember you didn't fall in love with a job, but with a man. A few paltry dollars, or even a lot of paltry dollars is not worth the price of hurting that wonderful guy who makes your heart beat faster! (A heart beating faster with love is not nearly as dangerous as is blood pressure being raised by malice!)

What
Can
I Do?

After coming to terms with self and family, the next logical question is, "What can I do?" After praying about a course of action and honestly answering the questions in Chapter 1, you may by now have some idea of the type of work most suitable for you and your lifestyle.

KINDS OF HOME BUSINESSES

Basically, all types of work fall into three categories: teaching, selling, and service. Yet under each classification there are endless possibilities and variations. You may even have a home business which simultaneously covers more than one category.

Betty James, of Doraville, Georgia, enjoyed her hobby of decorative painting so much that she soon had a house full of beautiful accessories. Friends who admired her work began asking Betty to paint articles for them, too. They brought her such things as old bread trays, umbrella stands, and even coal scuttles. Skillfully, Betty transformed the cast-offs into beautiful, one-of-a-kind accent pieces. She had performed a service.

As Betty's interest in decorative painting grew, she began selling some of her creations. These were items she had acquired, refurbished, and adorned with colorfully painted designs or scenes. Her home business had then branched out into the selling category, too.

Betty's skill increased as she produced more and more of her work. Consequently, other women often admired her finished products. Time after time she heard the remark, "Oh, I'd love to learn how to do that!" Again Betty made a transition. Now her home business includes teaching decorative painting to others.

While it's helpful to categorize types of home businesses in order to see the options available, it's also essential to keep an open mind regarding various possibilities for developing the business in more than one area. Had Betty James simply limited herself to one rigid category, she would have totally bypassed two other equally lucrative possibilities.

SELLING AS A HOME BUSINESS

Selling is possibly the most popular type of home business. The reason is simple. Many women develop a home business as a direct result of a hobby they love or a skill they already possess. If a woman enjoys her work, she will produce considerable output. After awhile the family cannot use any more hand-knitted sweaters, woven baskets, or blackberry jam. Consequently, in order to continue production, something must be done with the surplus. Selling comes about as a logical alternative. Then the creative woman has the continued pleasure of making her specialty, yet no longer has the guilty feeling of having overdone a good thing. Of course, the money is an incentive, too. After all, she reasons, selling an item for five dollars will keep her in raw materials sufficient to make eight more of the same object.

Even homemakers who are not remotely creative can find a profitable carreer in selling. If you haven't the slightest desire to make rag dolls or crocheted doilies, you can still have a home business in the selling field. There are innumerable items you can buy and resell for a profit if selling interests you, but creating does not.

Selling requires more face-to-face contact with more people than does either teaching or performing a service. Performing a service, such as making a dress for someone, involves meeting people, but in different circumstances. You'll usually meet the customer, work out the details of the service to be performed, do the job, and then report back to the one who hired you. This is one-to-one contact, but on a more prolonged basis and in a situation where you have a chance to get to know your customer. Selling may not always offer that advantage. While you may develop a stream of repeat customers, many selling jobs will be on a one-time basis only.

Because you may have only a brief time to present both yourself and your product, an easy-going manner of dealing with customers is essential. If meeting strangers puts butterflies in your stomach, selling might not be the right career for you. A successful career in selling depends on presenting both yourself and your product in a positive manner. You may be offering the world's most useful gadget for sale, but unless you can properly deal with people, success will be limited.

Selling usually involves considerably more paper work than does either teaching or service jobs, so a good bookkeeping system is essential. If you perform a service, such as typing manuscripts, your bookkeeping will be limited to keeping records of expenditures such as paper and supplies, and income received. A home business which involves selling requires more bookkeeping effort. You must record expenses for raw material, advertising, and mileage. You may also have postage expense. Additionally, you must collect a sales tax if your product is sold retail, and, of course, accurate records must be kept on the sales tax. If you sell wholesale in quantity lots, you may get involved with credit and billing, too. Nevertheless, don't let all the paper work scare you away from a career in selling. Even if you failed high school math, there's no need to panic. Your bookkeeping doesn't have to meet professional standards; it merely has to be accurate.

SERVICE JOBS

Service jobs offer a great deal of flexibility. First, you have the advantage of not having to cope with a large inventory of items. Most service jobs will involve simply you and perhaps one piece of equipment, such as a sewing machine, typewriter, or weaving loom. These may entail a considerable cash outlay in the beginning, but after the initial expense of acquiring your necessary equipment, most service jobs don't require large investments.

In my case, with a home sewing business, the purchase of the sewing machine was the only really big dent in my budget. After that, such things as keeping my scissors sharpened and giving the sewing machine an occasional oiling were about the only expenditures I had. These costs, plus the cost of the tiny amount of electricity used, were so small, I practically ignored them when tallying operational expenses.

Service jobs offer perhaps the greatest opportunity for building repeat business. If your business is poodle grooming and you are reasonably competent at the task, the same customers will need you again and again. Selling a tangible object such as a basket or a piece of pottery does not offer you this advantage. No matter how much a customer likes your product, she'll eventually get all of it she needs. Not so with a service—Fido will go right on needing your grooming services year after year.

Another advantage of service jobs is that if you are housebound because of small children, a physical handicap, or the lack of a car, you can still get your work done. While selling will involve occasional trips to buy supplies or to make deliveries to your customers, with a service job customers come to you.

You may find that customers enjoy watching you perform your service, too. If you can talk while you work, a service job can be a perfect opportunity for socializing while you get paid. Also, people appreciate your work more when they know how much effort went into the task. A customer who watches you hand-quilt only a small portion of her quilt top in an hour's time and sees how slowly the work goes, is less likely to quibble over prices. Then, too, customers are impressed when they see you re-do a job in order to get it exactly right for them. When I was sewing for others, I always insisted that customers try on finished garments before paying for them and taking them home. If the fit wasn't just right, I made the necessary adjustments right then. Certainly, the corrections took time, but the good will created was well worth the effort. Customers will come back again and again once they see that you take pride in your work.

16

Bookkeeping for a service job will mostly involve keeping an accurate record of income. Unless your service is one such as Betty James's, which involves the purchase of paint, you won't have much expense to record.

The biggest pitfall in a service business is failure to get payment from the customer. If you're selling a product, theoretically, you can march over to the nonpayer's house and ask to have the goods returned, but once a service job is done you must collect payment immediately, or you may never see any money at all.

TEACHING

Teaching is both selling and service. The salable product is knowledge and the service is giving it to others. Therefore, since teaching is a form of selling, enthusiasm is a necessary partner to knowledge. You can't "sell" someone else on the joys of creating jewelry unless you're "sold" on it yourself.

A mention of teaching makes most people think of college degrees and children. However, children aren't the only ones benefitting from the home business of teaching, and most of the courses being taught don't require college degrees. As a matter of fact, you can be so uneducated that you can neither read nor write, yet if you have a unique skill that's in demand, you can teach.

Teaching can consist of any subject from herb gathering to making corn husk dolls. A look at the courses offered by your local recreation center, community college, or YWCA will give you an idea of the subjects in which potential students are interested. In my community the junior college offers such things as photography, tax preparation, will preparation, creative writing, canning and freezing techniques, how to make Christmas decorations, and even how to become a clown or a magician! Evidently these subjects continue to attract students year after year because in the three years I've been on the mailing list the subjects offered have changed very little. Take a look at what is being offered in your community. Chances are you're qualified to teach at least one subject which is already a proven winner.

If standing in front of a crowd makes your knees go wobbly with fright, you can still find a way to teach. Try tutoring on a one-to-one basis. Anything that can be taught on a classroom basis can be taught equally well to only one student at a time. The main difference is that you won't make as much money. In order to realize a decent hourly wage you'll have to charge each student considerably more than you would in a classroom situation.

The biggest disadvantage to teaching may be that it intrudes into your privacy. For some reason, students in an informal classroom are much more likely to call the teacher on the telephone or to drop in for an unannounced visit. They don't really mean to intrude, but when they don't understand something you're teaching, they expect you to bail them out of their troubles. You might partially eliminate this problem by making yourself available to answer questions immediately after class.

Bookkeeping is not difficult when you are teaching. Unless you are also selling raw materials to your students (a highly profitable business—often more profitable than the classes are) your bookkeeping will consist mainly of entering into your records the fees received and deducting the cost of any demonstration materials.

BUT WHICH SHALL I CHOOSE?

With all the possibilities available to you in each of the three categories, are you wondering how you'll ever make a decision on the one that's right for you?

Let's take another look at your personal needs and interests. Have you determined how many hours per week you want to spend on your business? Obviously, if time is severely limited, your choice will have to be either teaching or performing a service. It's difficult to produce a product and make sales calls on a schedule limited to a few hours each week.

Have you also taken into account your temperament? If your patience is limited, try something besides tutoring or doing detailed work. If your shyness is extreme, find something which won't constantly bring you into contact with strangers.

LOOKING FOR A BUSINESS

Make a list of all your talents, skills, work experiences, and hobbies. Even if you are not especially proficient in a particular area, put that skill down on your list. For instance, if you play the piano fairly well, even though you've not had extensive training, put piano playing on your list. You might not have the ability to teach concert playing techniques, but you might be able to teach first-year students or even adults who wish to learn just enough music to be able to sing in the church choir. List everything you can think of that has any possibilities at all as a moneymaker.

As you complete your list of capabilities, you may be wondering how a group of unrelated skills could possibly lead to finding a home business. Yet the list is probably not as unrelated as it at first appears to be.

Let's suppose your list looks something like this:

1. sewing ability
2. management ability
3. enjoyment of meeting new friends
4. quilt-making as a hobby

Do you see a pattern emerging from these seemingly unconnected items? With a list like this you could exercise your talents in several ways. You might find it suitable to open a small shop in your home to sell quilting supplies to other quilters. If there is no room for a shop, perhaps making guilts to be sold on consignment might be the answer. If meeting people is a pleasure, you might enjoy taking a booth in arts and crafts fairs to provide yourself with an opportunity to make new acquaintances while bringing in extra income. However, if all forms of selling are uninteresting to you, a service job might be appealing. Many potential customers would like to find a qualified quilter to finish their own hand-pieced quilt tops. Then to carry your range of qualifications to all possible fields, you might decide this list of skills and interests points in the direction of teaching.

Look at your own list in this way and soon you will see a definite pattern emerging from seemingly unrelated components.

How,
Where,
and How Much?

FINDING WORK SPACE

By this time, you may have some potential business in mind but have begun to wonder where to put it. Although six family members occupying space in a three-bedroom ranch house with no basement doesn't leave mommy much operating area, ingenuity will come up with some workable arrangement. Although the dining room table may temporarily suffice as your work space, you'll never be quite as productive in a family traffic area as in a place where relative privacy can be achieved. When you set up your work area, try to make it a permanent part of your life. Too many homeworkers begin their new career with makeshift arrangements only to discover five years later that all their income is being spent on other things and those hoped for improvements never came to pass.

If it's impossible to find a corner to call your own, then at least be strict with yourself and use those first earnings only for upgrading your work area. It's a waste of time and energy to have to pack away your tools every time you need space for family activities. The only way to be consistently productive is to locate a spot where you can, when necessary, leave everything out and close the door on the clutter.

EQUIPMENT NEEDED

Another basic need for a successful home business is an honest evaluation of costs. No matter what you teach, create, or sell, certain expenses will cut into your profits. The cost may be small, such as a soft drink for the child you tutor after school each day, or large, such as forty-nine dollar wood frames for your oil paintings; but nevertheless, all businesses involve *some* expense. Sometimes the expense is constant and has to be taken into account for each item you produce. In other cases the business will entail putting out a substantial cost in the beginning, such as buying a typewriter or a sewing machine.

If your proposed endeavor involves the purchase of some kind of expensive equipment, consider renting what you need for the first few weeks. It would be somewhat annoying to discover two weeks after buying a nine hundred dollar typewriter that you hated the home typing business and could not tolerate another second of it.

Although the cost of renting the equipment you need may seem like money thrown out the window, try to look at both sides of the picture. It's better to waste a few dollars per week on rent rather than risking a more substantial amount on the purchase of equipment that might not be used more than a few times. Renting also gives you the chance to try several models so that by the time you are ready to buy, you'll know exactly what you want. Then you won't have to spend the next thirty years being silently reproached by the sight of some dust covered, unused gadget stuffed into a corner of your home.

Whenever you do get ready to buy your equipment, try to find out exactly what you will be doing with it *before* you spend your money. I made a mistake in that department myself. I bought an expensive sewing machine for my home sewing business and paid thirty dollars extra for a monogram attachment because I was certain that orders for monograms would pour in. However, in the five years I've owned the sewing machine I've done only four monograms—all for my own family, not for paying customers. I forgot to take into account that during the time *before* I had a monogrammer no one had once asked for that service. Admittedly, my foresight was bad, but in this case my hindsight wasn't too clear either. A more realistic appraisal of my sewing business could have saved me thirty dollars.

SUPPLIES

The other type of expense you'll incur is the all-the-time cash outlay for supplies. for instance, if you are producing decoupaged plaques, you'll be constantly buying wood, designs, glue, and finish. The only way to cope profitably with all this expense is to find a wholesale supplier and to buy in large enough quantities to persuade the wholesaler to deal with you. You cannot make a decent profit buying what you need from a retailer.

Sometimes finding a wholesale supplier is somewhat difficult because your friendly, neighborhood retailer is not inclined to undermine his own profits by telling you where to get your materials cheaper. However, you can go to the library and look up the address of the company which makes what you need (look in the *Thomas Register of American Manufacturers*) and write directly to them, asking for their wholesale prices. Even if they are not agreeable to selling the small amount you need (ten dozen doesn't look small to you, but it does to them!), they may be able to give you the name of a supplier who can fill your order at discount prices. If you don't have the slightest idea where to obtain the supplies you need, try looking in magazines that appeal strictly to specialized audiences. For instance, did you know there are specialized magazines for doll collectors, model railroad fans, and quilt-makers? All of these magazines carry ads from suppliers who stock the kind of specialized items you will be needing. Look in the library copy of *Writer's Market* to obtain addresses of magazines which are not carried on the newsstands.

In buying supplies, as in buying equipment, go slowly at first. If you later decide you don't want to continue the particular business you initially chose, you won't be left with a large quantity of material you can't use. When my daughter was small, I made clothes for eleven-inch fashion dolls. Eventually I grew tired of all those itsy-bitsy garments, and now I'm left with tiny snaps, sparkly sequins, and miles of rickrack. It really *is* better to buy in small quantities at first, even if you do have to pay a somewhat higher price for your initial investment in raw materials. Then, after establishing your business, you can go to the more profitable quantity wholesale buying.

PRICING

One of the most puzzling things about a home business is the determination of how much to charge. I've encountered many homeworkers who had all the orders they could handle, but while production was gigantic, profits were miniscule. Too many homeworkers make the mistake of underpricing their work. Unfortunately, once you set a price and begin selling a product, it is almost impossible to raise prices. Customers react negatively to price hikes.

If you are willing to work for slave wages, most customers are perfectly willing to let you do so. Even your best friend will probably let you make her a dress for five dollars or keep her child for ten dollars a week if those are the ridiculous prices you quote. After all, she assumes you are in business to make money, and she supposes you know what you are doing when you set your price.

Eventually, if you underprice your efforts, you will begin to feel put upon as you discover profits are not rolling in as you had optimistically anticipated. Then you will feel foolish and maybe even resentful of those whom you feel have taken advantage of you. The result: friendships will likely be tossed out along with your home business.

The best solution is to set prices high enough in the beginning. *Never, never, never* work cheaper for one customer than for another. Regardless of who the customer is, let the price be the same for all. Otherwise word will get around and those who are paying full price will either resent your partiality and will stop buying, or else they, too, will ask for the lower price. No matter how close the friendship is, don't make exceptions. If a person is truly your friend she will respect your integrity and will want to compensate you for your time and effort. After all, you are running a business, and it ought to be conducted in a businesslike manner. Your customers shouldn't be allowed to bargain with you any more than they would with the cashier at the supermarket. The only exception might be if you decide to trade goods or services. (This is not a lowering of your prices.) There are times when you get more value for your work by swapping something of yours for things other than cash.

COST EVALUATION

What is a realistic price to charge for your goods and services? The first step might be to look around your neighborhood and find out what others with similar businesses are charging. Suppose someone else is creating an article such as the one you have in mind and is selling it for twenty dollars. Does this mean you can sell yours for the same price? Actually, your competitor's price may not work at all for you. You also have to consider quality, distribution, and regular customers. Perhaps your competitor started her business years ago and since she's never raised her price, twenty dollars no longer provides her with much profit. Wouldn't it be a mistake to begin your business with a shoestring profit simply because she's willing to work that way? Suppose, on the other hand, that you have access to lower priced raw materials and can easily sell your product at eighteen dollars and still make a good profit. This ploy won't work as well as you might at first believe. Remember, if you can attract more customers by lowering the price to eighteen dollars, it's only a matter of time until some other enterprising person finds a way to cut the price to sixteen dollars. The best course of action is to start out with prices equal to or even higher than your competitors. But their price should not constitute your final decision.

To determine the best selling price in your own case, begin by writing down all costs involved, whether it be for equipment, raw materials, research, advertising, gasoline, or professional membership fees. Then calculate how long it will take to produce the article or service. Be as realistic and honest as possible in your assessment. For instance, if you are baby-sitting, even though you must stay constantly alert to the child's needs, you can simultaneously do other chores. Naturally, if you clean house, sew, or cook at the same time you are baby-sitting, the job should not command as high a price as a job that does not allow you to also do other activities at the same time. A job such as typing, which requires total concentration and cannot be done at the same time as anything else, will require a higher fee.

If you plan to produce a product which can be made assembly line fashion, it's still imperative to determine exactly how long it takes to make just one. Include in your time estimate such things as trips to the store for supplies and time spent in designing, packing, and billing.

Perhaps after adding all these costs the final figure is such that you are certain no one would pay that much. Consider how much money you could reasonably expect to make if you took a public job doing whatever you are trained to do. Using a realistic figure as your estimated salary, deduct such things as bus fare, lunches, babysitter fees, extra clothing, and convenience foods. Now look again at your results. Wouldn't you have to make a gross of more than six dollars an hour just to be able to bring home three dollars for an hour's work? Then consider that the homeworker has few of the expenses of the woman with a public job. Accordingly, even if you make *less* with a home business than with a public job, you may actually wind up with *more*. With this thought in mind, readjust your estimated price for your home-produced goods or services and you should arrive then at a fair price to charge.

PRICE CHANGES

Perhaps you also worry about overpricing. This is not something you will have to worry about for very long. If your prices are too high, people will let you know. Either they will come right out and tell you or else they will not buy your product or service. It's always better to start out with slightly higher prices, especially if you are planning to have the same customers again and again. After a customer gets accustomed to buying your product or service, she will not be pleased to have you go up on the price. Inevitably, bad feelings will result if you do.

Another alternative is a printed price list with the notation in *large* letters: "These prices are in effect only until December 31." Customers won't become nearly as upset over price changes if they've had advance warning about them.

There's one puzzling thing about pricing, and if you stay in business long enough you'll eventually have a chance to wonder about it. No matter how much you charge, there are inevitably some people who view price as the only criteria of quality. It's hard to understand people who turn up their noses at a product marked "$10.00," but buy half a dozen of the same product if the price is doubled. It sounds unbelievable, but it's true!

Do Your
Homework

The chief reason for the failure of most unsuccessful home businesses is the lack of effective preplanning. Mostly preplanning boils down to one vital question: Is there a market for the product, service, or skill? Regardless of how hard you work, how meticulous your bookkeeping is, or how cooperative your family is—you can't make money without customers.

IS THERE A MARKET?

After coming to a conclusion about the kind of business you want to operate, take a look at your neighborhood and town. What kind of community do you live in? Is it a suburban haven for young families or is it a retirement village for the over-sixty set? Is it an industrial area, farming community, or a place from which workers commute? What's the typical income class—lower, middle, or upper? Is it an area conservative in outlook and tradition or is it an area with a personality of "let's try anything that's new?" All these factors are going to influence your success in both subtle and obvious ways.

If your neighbors are mostly retired folks they may not eagerly sign up for your karate classes, but more likely would be interested in such things as art, photography, or even foreign language classes. Likewise, if you're selling a craft, retired people may be less likely to buy. Remember, they have plenty of leisure time to create their own crafts. Also, they may be living on fixed incomes which make them less likely to buy luxury items.

If, however, you are still thinking about that karate class and you live in a community where teen-agers abound, then your idea could very well be a winner. But in a neighborhood like that, you probably couldn't do too well with needlepoint classes!

WHAT'S THE COMPETITION?

As you look around your community, you may notice others are engaged in the same business you are thinking about starting. In this case, you'll need to assess realistically the situation in order to determine if the area is capable of supporting all of you. If the product or service you are planning to offer is popular enough, the fact that there is competition should not scare you away from the market. In fact, if the other businesses are extremely successful, the proprietors may even welcome you gladly.

When I began my home sewing business, I knew no other women who were doing that sort of work. Yet, as a result of my newspaper ad, several other seamstresses called me. I would have supposed they would not welcome competition, but on that point I was wrong. Each one who called me was happy to know I was starting a home sewing business. Rather than being discouraging to me, the five callers boosted my optimism considerably. Each of the ladies offered to send me some of her surplus business! As I later learned, a seamstress who can effectively sew for others *always* has more business than she can handle. As a result, it's to her advantage to locate other seamstresses to whom she can refer frantic customers who simply *must* have a special occasion dress made right away. The six of us never met each other in person, yet over a period of three years we constantly helped each other. (We also warned each other of customers to avoid—individuals who were too hard to please, who failed to keep fitting appointments, or who grumbled over prices.)

Although it is a wonderful experience to develop a circle of friends with the same home business as yours, you must also be prepared for competitors who are not so friendly. One woman told me of her encounter with a competitor who thought the field was not big enough to support two businesses. Using very unladylike language, the competitor denounced the new businesswoman.

Whether or not the competition receives you with open arms, both of you can successfully operate as long as you don't make the fatal mistake of trying to undercut each other's prices. That's a rapid route to failure. If you must compete, do so by offering a greater range of products or services, or by offering better quality or more convenient business hours. Price wars don't accomplish any lasting results for either business. Volume alone does not insure profits. One hundred customers a day won't put money in the bank if you're not making any money from the transactions.

DO I HAVE A WORKABLE BUSINESS PLAN?

While the great majority of home businesses start out being conducted on the family's dining room table with a minimum of money and planning, the best approach is to start your business, no matter how small it is, in the same businesslike manner you would start a giant corporation.

When a would-be entrepreneur wants to start a business and has no capital to do so, he or she finds it necessary to borrow money from a bank. In order to protect its investment, the bank will usually require the borrower to present a written, carefully detailed plan of action called a business plan.

Of course, most home businesses won't begin by borrowing money, but if you really want to get a clear idea of where you're going with the business, preparing a written business plan for your own use may help you locate your strengths and weaknesses *before* investing your time and money.

Here's how a business plan is prepared:

1. Determine what your goals, both immediate and long-range, will be.

2. Calculate your estimated necessary money needs.

3. Describe the competition and its strengths and weaknesses.

4. Devise a workable plan for obtaining raw materials at the lowest possible price from a reputable dealer.

5. Make a notation of any legal problems or any government restrictions you might encounter such as zoning ordinances and health rules.

6. List all tax responsibilities.

7. Show exactly how you propose to start the business.

8. Decide what you'll do about credit buying and selling.

9. Determine the form your business will take. Will you work alone, hire some help, recruit free labor from your family, or ask a friend or relative to go into partnership with you?

10. Write down all possible hindrances and obstacles you already know you are likely to encounter. While you obviously can't anticipate everything, it is helpful to have a "battle plan" ready for the anticipated inconveniences.

11. Decide on a tentative selling price.

Most women who are planning a home business will groan over my suggestions of a written business plan and maybe even mutter, "Oh, that's too much trouble. I'm only planning to work four hours a week and make about twenty dollars. I don't need to go to all that trouble." Yes, you do! No matter how simple the home business you plan to start is, developing a workable business plan *first* will make the road to success smoother for you. Besides, if your business is *that* simple, you can probably draw up a business plan in less than ten minutes. Would you deny your business ten minutes that might lead to hours and hours of saved time later?

HOW CAN I TEST THE MARKET?

In the world of big business, no corporation would ever put a product on the market without first conducting extensive tests to see if the public is likely to be receptive to that product. Before investing millions of dollars in production, the corporations try to determine if the product is salable. Whether the product is dog food or deodorant, you can be sure any item you see on a store shelf did not appear there without first being tested thoroughly. Often years are spent in testing before a product finally makes its appearance on the market.

Of course, you don't have the resources of the big business world, but still the idea of testing the market can work for you, too. When you do a market test, you create your product or service on a small scale, distribute it to a selected audience, and carefully note all reactions. This gives you a reasonably accurate idea of the kinds of changes which need to be made in order to make the product more successful.

To show you how this can work for you, even on a limited scale, I'll explain how I did market research on rag dolls.

First, I made a model of the doll I wanted to produce. I carefully recorded costs and time involved. Then I presented the doll to my four-year-old daughter. That was the quality and endurance test. After watching Karen play with the doll for a week or so, I had a reasonably good idea of some changes that needed to be made in the design. Since the doll was the type to appeal to young children, I noticed my first error was in the doll's size—it was a bit too large to be comfortably handled by preschoolers. The second thing that needed changing was the method used for fastening the clothes. Buttons are difficult for youngsters. Then, since four-year-olds can put a great deal of stress and strain on a beloved doll, I realized the stress points of the seams needed to be double-sewn for durability. Also, the hair, which was applied by hand, was not sewn on strongly enough to withstand the "mommy's" favorite way of carrying her "baby"—by the pigtails. Consequently, I devised an original method of using the sewing machine to apply the hair. Favorite dolls enjoy a great deal of traveling and Mama Goose (that was the doll's name!) soon needed a bath. Since the cotton batting she was stuffed with dried slowly, I realized lightweight nylon stockings would be a better stuffing material.

After doing my product research, I turned to market research. Karen took Mama Goose with her everywhere we went, and I listened to remarks people made about her. When asked if I would make dolls to sell, I quoted a price. Through trial and error and public opinion, I finally arrived at a price acceptable to both my customers and myself. Then to further test the market, I let Karen use some of my dolls as gifts when she went to birthday parties. The comments of the little guests and their mothers gave me further insight into marketing my craft.

The "research" I did was on a very elementary level, but I'm using this example to show you that even a very simple product should be thoroughly tested for durability, salability, and profit potential *before* you plunge into business too deeply to make necessary changes.

To further test your market, you can try advertising on a limited scale and coding your ads to determine which ones are serving you most effectively. For instance, suppose you are selling birdhouses and you decide to advertise in two magazines. Since you want to get the most possible return for your advertising dollars, you'll need to know which ad brings in the most responses.

Let's pretend there are magazines entitled *Bird Lovers* and *Feathered Friends*. To gauge response to ads placed in these two publications, code the ads in this way: use the same name and address in both places, but as part of your ad in *Bird Lovers* use the code "Dept. BL." For your ad in *Feathered Friends* use the code "Dept. FF." In this way when orders come in you'll be able to judge which periodical is generating the best market for your product.

It's even possible to do market research on service jobs. As a matter of fact, since most service jobs will require an expensive investment in some sort of equipment, market research will save you a considerable amount of money—especially if the service business does not turn out to be feasible.

Let's consider the possibilities of market testing a service job which often comes to mind when women start thinking about making extra dollars at home. Typing as a home business often seems a profitable endeavor. Yet, there is a home typing job which is much more profitable than regular typing and not much more difficult. The job is composing type for printers, and the work is done on a machine similar to a typewriter. Since getting started in this type of work can be expensive, a reliable market test will give you a good idea of your chance for success before you involve yourself financially.

The first step, of course, is to contact several print shops and ask if they have a need for free-lance work. If not, there is no need to pursue the matter further. If so, after locating several sources of potential income, you'll need a machine. A composing machine is very expensive—in the thousands—so obviously you can't rush right out and buy one. The answer: Market test by renting your machine, learning the trade, and building up your business. If your market test for some reason shows that this venture is not going to work out profitably, you're only out your time and the cost of one month's rent on the machine.

Marketing research is not some ominous stumbling block to your business, but an invaluable tool for helping you present the best possible product or service in the most *profitable* manner.

Getting Started in the Crafts Business

CRAFTS AS A BUSINESS

When homemakers start thinking about making a few extra dollars with a home job, it seems thoughts inevitably turn to making and selling crafts. At first glance, crafts seem the perfect solution to the extra money dilemma. After all, the enterprising homemaker reasons, I already make things in my spare time, people are fond of things that are handmade, and besides, I just love doing handicrafts. Making money with what I create is going to be the simplest thing in the world. Isn't that right?

To answer that question honestly and precisely, I must reply, Yes, of course—and no, absolutely not!

Any craftswoman who has successfully created and marketed a product learned—usually the hard way—that making handcrafted items to sell is not remotely similar to making items merely for pleasure. While hopefully the selling craftswoman *does* find pleasure in her craft, at the same time she must realize that creating crafts as a business endeavor requires a business approach.

THE BUSINESS OF PLEASING OTHERS

The first surprise the craftswoman encounters is that others may not like the same colors and designs she finds pleasure in. Nevertheless, the successful selling craftswoman reconciles herself to creating what sells rather than only what pleases her. Of course, this does not mean that principles or quality are to be sacrificed, but rather that flexibility becomes an important ingredient in any design. Although she may feel that beige is the best or only color appropriate for macramé purses, she will find many potential customers are equally sure purple, or orange, or chartreuse is the right color.

The second surprise for the craftswoman is found in her statement that "everybody likes handmade items." First of all, there's not one thing in this world that *everybody* likes, and, even if they did, sales aren't guaranteed on that basis alone. Crafts, like everything else, go in and out of style. In the fifties, you probably couldn't have given away a macramé purse, much less sold one, but little sets of costume jewelry scatter pins were a hot item. Now, purses are "in," and the selling craftswoman who formerly made sequined poodle pins is struggling to learn the difference between a square knot and a half-hitch.

To further complicate matters, craft shops have discovered that teaching crafts to customers sells more supplies. Now everybody seems to want to get in on the popularity of crafts. Years ago craft techniques were secrets closely guarded by craftspeople. Now everybody has access to learning practically any craft imaginable. Craft books fill the libraries and even a fumble-fingers may find it more enjoyable to create her own items rather than buy them from you. Just because there are no women within a hundred miles of you selling your product, there is no guarantee you can sell it if, at the same time, every homemaker with five minutes of spare time is producing the item to give away. A craft can actually be too "in" to be salable.

What about the other basis for going into the crafts business? "I already make things in my spare time," you said. How much spare time? Have you calculated how much time a crafts career will take? A half hour a day spent doing needlepoint hardly constitutes a valid involvement in spare time crafts. The woman who seriously plans to make money with her business can't do crafts in a few minutes of spare time. She must have the ability to create time for craft work by getting organized and going to work. In some ways, making time for craft work is more difficult than is making time for a service type of home business. If you are teaching or baby-sitting or typing, the pupil or baby or blank envelopes are right there demanding your attention. On the other hand, it's easier to ignore crafts or to even feel guilty about doing them. We can rationalize typing as "work" and can even feel virtuous about getting with it and doing a good job. Crafts, however, are "fun," so even if you plan to make money from your craft projects, it's easy to put them aside in favor of other household duties.

SETTING PRIORITIES

First, you must think of the craft business as *business* and approach it in the same manner as any other money making endeavor. You cannot be a successful selling craftswoman with a "when I feel like it" or a "when I get around to it" attitude. The successful crafts businesswoman creates when she has a headache, when it is a beautiful day for gardening, when one hundred-one interruptions come, and even when it's her birthday, if she has orders to fill.

Although a Christian woman must always put her family ahead of any moneymaking project, she is, nevertheless, committed to keeping her word once she gives it. A craftswoman who cannot deliver what she promised to the consignment shop or to the individual customer is going to discover her business is going downhill. Once you take the plunge and become a business woman, customers expect professionalism. People can understand if you have a family emergency and can't deliver once or maybe even twice, but customers are not going to understand if you consistently have excuses. The best policy is to be so conscientious that your track record will be your own best reference when a time comes that you honestly can't deliver as promised. When your son breaks his arm, or your mother-in-law arrives unexpectedly, or your dog has twelve puppies in the living room, you'll find that customers to whom you've already shown your reliability may be surprisingly understanding.

Realizing that your crafts undertaking is a *business* will also give you the confidence to not only respect your own work but to cause others to respect it, too. As Christians, we must always give our best effort. Moneymaking is a necessary part of this life, and while it should not become important beyond reason, it should be approached with the idea of representing Christ. If you allow customers to think of you as unbusinesslike or as a "pushover," they will not respect you nor will they be interested in hearing about the Christ you represent. Remember the parable of the talents? The unworthy servant who hid his talent in the ground actually did nothing blatantly dishonest. Yet, his unsuccessful approach to money management brought reproach on himself. You are not doing yourself or anyone else a favor by being less than businesslike in your transactions.

WHAT CAN I SELL?

Most craftswomen already know what they want to sell. Few actively set out to look for a salable craft but rather branch out from a hobby they already love. Yet, therein lies the problem. Most homemakers who are also craftswomen love crafts— plural. The dilemma is which one to choose for the crafts business. In reaching a decision about a craft to be offered for sale several factors should be considered:

1. *How much investment does it take to get started?* Some crafts, such as ceramics, may involve a large initial expenditure. However, it's not advisable to rush into such expensive undertakings without first being certain that the interest in the craft is a genuine one likely to last a lifetime and that the financial return from the investment will offset the expense. In the case of ceramics, it is expensive to pay someone else to do your firing, but while the market is being tested paying for the use of someone else's kiln could be a bargain. It would be a big mistake to start out by buying your own kiln only to discover later on that the business was not working out successfully for you. Another alternative is to find a craft similar to the one you are interested in but which can be done in a less expensive manner. For example, an alternative to ceramics is plastercraft which gives a somewhat similar effect and requires no firing. Practically any craft you can think of offers some sort of cheaper alternative.

2. *Would I buy this article if someone else were selling it?* Being objective about your crafts is about as easy as being objective about the beauty and intelligence of your children,

but the beginning handicrafter must at least try to be honest with herself. Surprisingly, many craftswomen get started in a business because they did buy something someone else had made. Then, because they liked the item so well they began making more for themselves. Yet determining the desirability of a craft is an evasive process. Such factors as cost, usefulness, color, fashion, and ingredients make the difference. Quality and uniqueness have to be considered, too. Try to see the craft as though it belonged to someone other than yourself. As honestly as possible, assess its attributes and shortcomings. If you see too many negative points which you, as a consumer, would notice, the project is probably not a worthwhile one.

3. What's the competition? Being the only maker of a product in the entire state does not guarantee success. Competition is not only other craftspeople who create the same product, it is also other products. Especially if your creation is a purely ornamental one, you are competing not only with people who make a similar ornamental product, but also with people who make a totally different product that is more a necessity than an ornament. You may have to compete with your customer's son's need for a new pair of shoes as well. Since ornamental crafts are usually impulse purchases your competition comes from all directions. If your craft is a multi-faceted one, you may even find yourself in competition with yourself. Most working craftspeople can tell you at least one sad story of how they offered a customer so many choices the customer became confused and actually bought nothing.

Perhaps the worst blow is the competition from the customer. You only have to work a booth at a craft fair for about five minutes before hearing somebody say, "You're charging *that* much for a little thing like that! There's nothing to it. I could make one of those without even trying." Whether or not the customer actually can make one is irrelevant. She thinks she can and you lose a sale.

4. Is the quality as good as I can make it? No product is going to be a continuing success if that product is not well made. Certainly, thousands of shoddily made handcrafted items have been sold, but consumers are not stupid. A poorly made item might sell initially, but eventually low quality workmanship will be the downfall of a crafts business. As Christians we must go beyond what is acceptable and reach for the goal of having each item we make represent our best efforts. Doing a quality job goes beyond doing merely what we can get by with doing. Quality in a handmade item counts even in the places customers can't see.

When I made rag dolls to sell, I always double-sewed the stress points. No one except me could tell because the stitching was inside the doll and never seen at all by the customers. Yet I had the satisfaction of knowing each doll I made could successfully endure all the tugging, dragging, and loving any little mother could dish out.

5. Can I make money with this craft? There is little point in going into business not to make money, yet some women seem to have this objective in mind! There is no profit in a business consisting of only expenditures and time and no earnings.

DECIDING ON A SELLING PRICE

What is a reasonable selling price for a handcrafted item? Only two people have the answer to that question—you and your customer. Ideally, the selling price should give you a reasonable profit for the time and materials invested and at the same time not put too much strain on the customer's bank account. Hardly anyone can resist a bargain. Most people want to feel as if they have made a shrewd purchase. Therefore, what must a craftswoman take into consideration when setting a purchase price? The price must be high enough to give the seller a profit, yet low enough to attract customers.

1. What do the materials cost? While the cost of the necessary raw materials may fluctuate (usually upward!), the basic kinds of ingredients remain the same. For instance, when making rag dolls, I always needed cotton fabric, embroidery floss, rug yarn, and stuffing. Yet, the first rag doll I made cost me five dollars to make, while the last one I made for the consignment shop cost only thirty-five cents. Why the large discrepancy in costs? I learned, between the first doll and the last, to cut corners on expenses. I learned that it is not possible to buy all materials at full price from a craft store and still make a profit. I eventually learned to use my head instead of my bank account. For example, the first rag doll was cut precisely according to pattern directions, each bit of cloth bought exactly for that purpose and in specified amounts, and the stuffing purchased as the pattern dictated. Obviously a ten-dollar doll (this was in 1971) that cost five dollars to make leaves *no* profit for the creator. Consequently, I had to cut cost. A garment factory allowed me to cart away—free!—fabric scraps. Certainly tons of them were the wrong color, but in every batch were usable scraps of flesh color, blue stripes, red checks, solid white, and other colors I needed. Then a friend told me about a hosiery shop which used those old-fashioned leg mannequins to display the various shades of hosiery for sale. When the hosiery came off display it was discarded. Guess who got the discarded hosiery—free? It was better for stuffing the dolls because it was lightweight, fluffy, and totally washable—a fact mothers of small children appreciate. By eliminating overhead I increased my profits on each doll by $4.65.

You, too, can perhaps find similar ways of cutting the costs of your materials. While there is a limit to how much a customer will pay for a craft item, her opinion of the worth of the object will remain the same whether your raw materials cost five dollars per unit or thirty-five cents. Therefore, since the materials cost is one of the primary considerations in selecting a selling price, cut costs as much as possible in order to achieve a price acceptable to your customers. Slashing the cost of materials is one of the most effective ways of keeping your price within the customer's buying limit and within your own expectations of profit.

2. How long does it take to make this product? A craftswoman frequently does work for less than the minimum hourly wage, but still there must be some reasonable compensation for the effort expended. Therefore, it is advisable that you try the assembly line method of construction as a possible timesaver.

When I made doll clothes to sell, everyone was astonished at the speed with which I could produce an entire Barbie wardrobe. What was my secret? Assembly-line style cutting and sewing speeded the process immensely. I stacked up several layers of fabric, and, depending on the thickness of the cloth, cut from two to five garments with one swipe of the scissors. At the sewing machine, I ran the garments through one after the other, never cutting the thread between pattern pieces, but always letting one piece feed into the sewing machine directly at the end of the previous seam. In this manner, I could produce a wardrobe in about three hours.

If assembly line methods can be used with your craft, your output will be considerably greater. The time saved in "manufacturing" is the same as extra dollars tacked on to the selling price.

3. What does it cost to market this product? Too many handicrafters figure materials and labor cost and forget that the advertising, display expense, delivery costs, postage, entrance fees, and driving time and expense must also be worked into the asking price of the product. Even if your advertising consists merely of one newspaper ad and one stack of business cards, these costs must be figured into your price estimate. In addition, if you plan to exhibit at craft shows, you'll need color slides for the entrance committee to judge your work.

The display center you choose might be as simple as a card table or a few planks stacked together, but nevertheless it is an expense and must be added to the selling price.

Some of the well promoted shows charge participants an entrance fee of twenty-five dollars or more. This cost also has to be taken into account.

Any cost, no matter how large or how small, must be calculated if you are to arrive at a satisfactory selling price which will give you more than pauper's wages.

4. Can I sell wholesale at this price? Professional full-time craftspeople consider wholesale selling as a vital part of the crafts business. Basically, craftspeople have two prices for their products. One price is what they charge customers who buy directly from them. The other price is for shops, galleries, and distributors who purchase craft products for resale. Your wholesale price must be low enough to encourage others to buy your work for resale, yet high enough to give you a fair profit even on wholesale. Also, you should not sell your own work cheaper than the shop sells it. Suppose you charge a shop ten dollars wholesale, and the shop markets your product for eighteen dollars. It isn't fair to the shop if at the same time you are selling the same kind of product all around town for twelve dollars. The shop owner shouldn't have to worry about being in competition with you. Choose a price you can both live with and then both of you can retail for the same price. After all, if he succeeds in getting eighteen dollars for the product, shouldn't you get that much also? The wholesale price should be your selling minimum—the lowest price you can sell at and still make a reasonable profit. Your retail price must take into consideration such things as handling and storage which are your problems only in retail sales and not in wholesale selling.

Other Ways to Sell Crafts

When most people think of selling crafts, their thought is usually of selling on a one-to-one basis. While this may be the most frequent and most satisfying method, other opportunities for selling exist, too.

IDEAS FOR CRAFT SALES

1. Consignment shops. Some stores will agree to exhibit your product and to obtain for you the price you have set. Many consignment shops deal exclusively with handcrafted items. Occasionally gift shops, florist shops, book stores and jewelry stores may also handle consignment selling on a more limited basis.

With consignment selling, the important point is to get your money at the time you deliver the craft to the seller. Although some shops work on the principle of having you bring in an item and if and when it sells you get your money, these stores should be dealt with on a last resort basis only. Preferably, the store should purchase your product outright. Most of the stores which don't purchase outright will ask you to sign an agreement stating that you will not hold the store responsible for loss or damage to your goods. If the article has not sold within three months, you will be required to go back and reclaim it. The disadvantage of this type of arrangement is obvious. You might have to waste time and gasoline driving back and forth several times to deliver and collect items without ever collecting any money for the time and effort expended.

As would be expected, the stores which purchase your goods outright have somewhat higher standards regarding the quality of the work which they will accept. Since the deal concludes when you leave the shop with the money, the proprietor will only buy items which he or she is confident will have the quality and appeal to be sure-fire sellers. Of course, getting your money right then and there is an added incentive to dealing with this type of merchant. In addition, once the article is purchased, you no longer have the worry of thinking about something disastrous happening to your work. If some ice cream covered, sticky child comes into the store, he's not your problem.

2. *Gift shops.* A few gift shops are receptive to the idea of purchasing items created by competent craftspeople. However, since gift shops generally carry items which are considered luxuries rather than necessities, gift shop customers tend to be people who are looking for unusual gadgets, novel gifts, and stylish decorative accessories. If you want to do this kind of selling, remember that quality in your product is a must, but originality goes a long way, too.

Do business only with shops which will allow you to attach to your product a small tag bearing your name. This helps to provide you with free publicity and to promote further sales. You cannot expect the gift shop to allow your address or phone number on the tag because repeat customers would come directly to you rather than to the shop. However, it is not at all unreasonable to ask to have your name identify your product. It doesn't hurt to build your reputation at the same time you're building your bank account.

Some shops may ask for exclusive rights to a particular design they are marketing for you. It is all right to let them be the exclusive distributor of a product if the terms are agreeable to both of you, but *never, never* sign anything giving away the rights to your own product. If someone else obtains all rights to your craft, he can not only hire others to produce it for him, but he can also legally stop you from making and selling your own original craft.

3. Specialty shops. Specialty shops are those which cater exclusively to one type of business. A candy store is a specialty shop and so is a book store. Specialty shops can be lucrative outlets for the handicrafter, but it does take some ingenuity to market in these areas. For instance, let's suppose you do leatherwork. What kind of specialty shops could market your wares for you? How about selling leather bracelets and pendants at a jewelry store, leather belts at a jeans store, leather pet collars at the pet store, leather purses at the shoe store, and leather book markers at the book store. With imagination, any product can be adapted to specialty shop use. You will find, however, that individually owned stores are more receptive to your ideas than are nationwide chain stores. As with gift shops, make certain any product you market through specialty shops carries your name.

4. Art galleries. If you thought some of the high quality gift shops were difficult to get into, perhaps you will be thoroughly intimidated by the thought of obtaining acceptance of your work by an art gallery. However, art galleries, like people, come in all varieties. Some are very formal and accept only items which are clearly *art* in the traditional sense of the word. Other galleries are more contemporary in outlook and define *art* in a more flexible manner.

The only way to judge whether your creation is more art than craft is by visiting several galleries and by observing what is proffered for sale by each one.

Galleries look for items unique in either materials, manner of using materials, or in statement. Depending on the creator and the raw materials and method of construction almost any craft can become art. Baskets, pottery, or quilts could be called crafts in the ordinary sense of the word. Yet, in the hands of a skilled worker, these same objects can be made to create an entirely different impression and thus become art.

In creating products to be sold on a one-to-one basis or in gift or consignment shops, the craftswoman usually produces in quantity the same type of item over and over again. This is not always the case when selling to galleries. Here the big selling point is often not "everybody has one," but rather "nobody else has one." It may be more difficult to get a start in gallery selling, but if you are producing a fine product you owe it to yourself to at least investigate all possibilities.

5. Kits and instructions. If people are forever asking how you do whatever it is that you are doing, you might find it a profitable undertaking to investigate the feasibility of letting the inquisitors pay for the privilege of asking. You can make up kits containing all the pieces necessary to assemble your product and you can package it with easily understood instructions. These kits should be priced at slightly below the price of your own finished product. For example, a $10.00 product might sell for $7.50 in kit form. For those who prefer to assemble their own components you might also offer a mimeographed or photo-copied set of instructions and/or patterns.

Craftspeople seem to have mixed emotions about giving away trade secrets. One group argues that every time you tell somebody else how to do your craft you are hurting your own selling chances. The other group argues that people who truly want to learn a craft are going to somehow find a way to do it whether you help them or not. Their reasoning is if competition is inevitable you might as well make money training the competition, too. Besides, the optimists say, the original craftsperson had a head start, and it will take the novice a long time to gain the same skill and reputation. Each craftswoman must make up her own mind about how she feels on the subject of giving away trade secrets. Perhaps the best solution would be to share general instructions, such as how to make candles, but to keep the specifics, such as how to make the one that's your trademark, to yourself.

6. Mail order. Crafts can be profitably sold by mail order but not in the manner you might expect. The best mail-order selling is that which is done as a result of your own mailing list of customers who have seen or bought your work previously. If you attend craft shows long enough and have enough spectators pocket your business card, eventually you'll get letters from people who saw your work and then after leaving the show regretted not buying one of your wares. This kind of mail-order selling works fine if: 1. You charge for the postage. 2. You charge a handling fee to cover cost of wrapping material, gasoline to drive the package to the post office, and insurance on the object.

7. Catalog sales. Selling a product through a promotional

catalog can be both a dream and a nightmare. On the plus side the promoter usually pays such expenses as printing, wrapping, and mailing. All you have to do is create and deliver. On the negative side, some promoters may ask you to kick in a few dollars to help pay for the privilege of being included.

Once you obligate yourself to catalog sales, you may find yourself becoming extremely bored with producing the same designs over and over. While galleries may require you to produce lesser quantities, or "limited editions," even the number required of one design may involve more repetition than you will want.

How do you get your craft featured in a catalog? Study the catalogs you like and then write a letter asking to have information on being included. You'll likely need a good set of slides to show the quality of your work. Then if the catalog's promoters express interest in your work, they'll ask to see a sample of the actual item.

8. *Craft fairs.* Inevitably, if you deal with handcrafted items long enough you'll find that selling your wares at craft shows is fun and likely very profitable. What could be more enjoyable than spending a day making money, meeting people, and enjoying the festive atmosphere of a country fair? (Don't pose questions like that to a seasoned veteran of the craft show circuit. She might tell you that at times poison ivy can be more fun than exhibiting at a craft fair!)

Basically, however, in spite of a few difficulties, craft shows can be extremely rewarding for a craftswoman, both financially and emotionally. A day of hearing customers ooh and aah over your wares can certainly boost your confidence in yourself and in your work.

ADVANTAGES OF CRAFT FAIRS

1. *Exposure.* You can't sell to people who don't know about your product, and one good fair can give you more exposure than you'll get in five years of selling to your friends and relatives. Selling is, of course, the object of the craft show game, but it is not the only benefit. Consignment shops and even galleries often send representatives to craft fairs to scout for prospective talent. Even if you don't immediately sell to them, the representative may be impressed enough with your work to

look you up at a later date and give you a chance. In addition, journalists and television and radio program directors like to do a bit of scouting at craft fairs, too, and they are looking for subjects and personalities to present to their readers, viewers, and listeners. Even a financially unsuccessful show can't be considered a total waste of time if you get some sort of publicity from it. Then, too, browsers sometimes take your business cards and may contact you months later to buy your product.

2. *Opportunity to meet other craftspeople.* While all the craftspeople at a fair are in direct competition with each other, it's rare to find craftspeople who will give you the cold shoulder. Many make a living solely from their crafts and consequently work fairs every week. Since they mingle with the same craftspeople over and over, many friendships are formed. You can learn more in one day spent with fellow crafters than you'll learn in a year of selling on your own. Crafters look out for each other, too. You'll find that the "oldtimers" can spot a shoplifter at a hundred paces and they'll tell you how to spot him, too. If you have to leave your booth they'll also watch to see that no one carries off your goods.

It pays to be a good listener when you go to craft fairs. You'll learn about shows, publications, organizations, and suppliers you never knew existed. Just use a little courtesy and learn what *not* to ask. It's certainly not Christ-like to use a friendship to gain information which will build your business and hurt your neighbor's.

Likewise, remember to be friendly and helpful, but don't give away your own trade secrets either. In two instances, I had "friends" take advantage of me this way. Once I told too many details about a business arrangement and a woman went to the retailer I was supplying and undercut my price. Another time I showed someone how to make a product which was my exclusive design. Guess which one of us made money and which one of us learned a valuable lesson on when *not* to tell everything. Proverbs 29:11 says, "A fool uttereth all his mind: but a wise man keepeth it in till afterwards."

3. *Opportunity to meet potential customers.* Meeting people is the essence of craft fairs. If you really don't enjoy talking to strangers, craft shows are not for you. The fair is for your financial benefit, but it's also for the customer's enjoyment. Therefore, it's up to you to see that the folks who come to your booth have a good time.

Be attentive to what customers say to you, and you'll be surprised how much you'll learn about human nature and about your own craft. People may give you clues to help you design a better product, and they also may teach you better ways of doing your work. Hobbyists who are interested in the same craft may be happy to tell you some short cut they've found or the name of some supplier whose prices are lower than the one you are using. Since they are not creating a product to offer for sale, many of them are not in competition with you and will freely share information. However, use caution here as in dealing with other selling craftspeople. Not all inquiries are as innocent as they sound.

4. *Money*. Yes, money is the big reason why craftspeople are so interested in participating in craft fairs. Why else would a handicrafter travel several hundred miles to sit in a dusty cornfield and swat flies and mosquitoes for two twelve-hour days? Craft shows are the selling craftsperson's bread and butter.

How much can you reasonably expect to make from a show? That's variable. It depends on you, your product, the neighborhood, the time of year, the kind of show you're in, the area where your booth is positioned, what your competitor is selling, and whether or not it rains.

One professional who works the good quality shows told me about a "good" fair she had experienced. She made fourteen hundred dollars selling five and ten dollar pieces of costume jewelry. Of course, this was not all profit. She had traveled three hundred miles to get to the show, had three nights motel bill to pay, had to buy ten meals, including the meals she ate on the traveling days, plus had to pay a twenty-five dollar entrance fee just to get into the show, where she spent twelve hours a day sitting in a booth. At the same time she also told me about the worst fair she ever had as a craft show participant. At that fair she took in only four hundred dollars for her efforts, yet her expenses were the same as they were at the good show.

"I never write off a show as a total loss," she says. "Even when it seems you've actually lost money, you can't always be sure. Sometimes you come home from a show all discouraged and then a few weeks later orders start pouring in from people who saw you but waited until later to buy."

DISADVANTAGES OF CRAFT SHOWS

1. Physical discomfort. In most cases the reward is worth the suffering, but anyone who thinks craft fairs are not 90 percent hard work, must be someone who has attended shows only as a spectator and not as a participator. The view from inside the booth is quite different from the view outside the booth. The hours are long, and, in spite of fatigue, the craftsperson must smile, demonstrate her work, and remain charming when there are more lookers than buyers and the lookers are sarcastic, surly, or snide. Twelve hours or more standing up can be hard on your back, legs, and feet. Therefore, comfortable shoes and nonbinding garments are vital. Outdoor shows are less tiring on your feet and legs than are shows held indoors on non-resilient floors. However, outdoor shows have other drawbacks—primarily the weather.

If you're exhibiting in the broiling sun (as you're most likely to be—the repeaters get the choice spots and the new kid on the block gets stuck in the frying pan position), a bad sunburn can accompany a day's work. And if you forget your hat, count on having a headache as a result of all that warmth beating down on your head.

Then there's the opposite side of the weather coin—rain. You *must* include water-proof coverings for yourself and your wares as part of your standard equipment. Of course, there's dreaded variety to the kinds of rain you may have to face. The all day drizzle that turns chilly and leaves your teeth chattering is the very worst because it makes potential customers either stay at home, or if they do show up, it makes them run by the exhibits so quickly there's no browsing and impulse buying. Sometimes rain brings along another undesirable companion—high winds. For this reason, you'll need to make certain your display has enough stability to withstand anything short of a hurricane. Also there's the kind of rain that doesn't slow down the customers but certainly works the craftspeople overtime. First, the weather gets so muggy and hot that the plastercrafts in the fair start acting like ceramics except that they fire themselves without benefit of a kiln. Then the rain comes in a heavy drenching downpour. You race frantically to cover your goods and by the time all the plastic is securely in place the torrent stops. This cycle repeats itself several times and when the day has ended, selling crafts at a fair no longer has its original appeal to you.

2. *People.* People are simultaneously the best and worst parts of craft fairs. You'll meet the friendly kind, the helpful kind, and, best of all, the buying kind. You'll also be called on to exercise your charm on the unfriendly, the rude, and, worst of all, the non-buying kind.

Talk to any exhibiting craftsperson for a while and you'll hear about the repertoire of remarks that make a craftsperson cringe:

"Isn't that cute!" (a nice compliment, but it loses its charm after the two-thousandth repetition).

"Your prices are too high."

"Is this made in Japan?"

"What do you call this stuff?"

"My grandmother used to have one of those."

"Give me your pattern. I want to make that myself."

"That's not so great. I can make one just like it."

"I bet you make a bundle with these little old things."

People! Where would the crafts business be without them?

HANDLING THE MECHANICS OF A CRAFT SHOW

1. *Transportation.* Unless you are selling something like rings or thimbles, it is going to be difficult to carry everything to a fair in the family car. Of course, if the show is local, you can solve the problem by making several trips, but if the show is out of town, you'll need more space than your car alone can provide. A van, truck, or even a camper is ideal, but unless you already have one of these or unless your craft business has been *very* profitable, you'll probably have to make do without benefit of owning anything more exotic than the family car. If you must have more room, rent a small utility trailer, which can be towed behind your car, or a roof-top carrier, which can offer quite a bit of extra storage space if your product is not too bulky.

The important thing is not to commit yourself to participate in any fair to which you are unable to conveniently transport yourself and your wares. You're in the business to make money, so if you pay a twenty-five dollar entrance fee only to become a "no show," you've defeated your purpose.

2. *Packing.* Packing is probably the dullest part of the crafts business, but good packing is one of the most vital ingredients. You can't sell broken pieces, so think of your profits and pack carefully.

Breakable items, such as pottery and ceramics, should be packed with ample newspaper as cushioning. This helps you and your customer because after a purchase customers expect *you* to figure out a way to get their pottery home in one piece.

Ultimately, if you stay in the crafts business long enough, you'll need a more convenient and permanent method of packing and transporting your wares. A cabinet-maker can build a carrying case exactly to your specifications, but a custom-made case is expensive, so be sure you know exactly what you need before putting down your money. The ideal case is one which transports, cushions, and displays your wares. If you can design a case which can be opened for display and then folded for carting the goods home, you will save yourself a great deal of time and effort by eliminating the packing and unpacking steps.

3. *Protecting.* It would be hard to say which kinds of goods are most troublesome to protect. Breakable things, such as pottery, carry a built-in risk. Cloth goods, especially those which appeal to children, are easily soiled. Small items, such as jewelry, are more susceptible to shoplifting.

To lessen the danger of breakage, don't leave anything near the display. This includes your lunch, extension cords, lawn chairs, and ice chests. If there's anything in sight to trip over, somebody will trip over it. Don't put the goods any closer than six inches from the front edge of the table. Pottery is safer when displayed on shelves. People tend to pick up and handle things that are placed on a table, but when wares are on a shelf, they don't get handled quite as much.

Don't be deluded into thinking you have the kind of goods which no one would steal. No matter what you make, somewhere, somebody will try to steal it. How can you protect yourself from shoplifting? First, take a helper along if possible. Two sets of eyes are better than one for spotting potential trouble. An old shoplifter's scheme is, "You keep her busy while I get the goods." Another way to lessen problems is by not displaying on all four sides. If you sit or stand at the back of the exhibit you can see as many as three sides, but no one can see behind herself.

The promoters of the craft fair should be willing to help with the security problems. Most of the higher quality fairs do hire guards to keep an eye on things. It's especially important that the show provide security if the show is scheduled for more than one day. Unless there is a night guard, you'll have to put up and take down everything in your display every day.

How can you keep your cloth goods from becoming soiled? First, you must accept the fact that some soiling is inevitable, particularly if you sell such items as dolls or stuffed animals. Some parents don't even try to restrain their children and even with parents who do try, there will occasionally be a child so quick as to wreak his damage faster than mama can say, "No! No!" The best method is diversion. Have some gimmick to use to attract a child's attention from what he can readily reach. Try placing your most valuable wares high enough to prevent them from being readily accessible.

Teaching

To many people, the word *teaching* stirs up mental images of chalkboards and children. Yet, a healthy portion of today's students are adults, the place of learning is not a traditional classroom, and the subjects being taught have nothing to do with the three R's.

WHAT DOES IT TAKE TO BE A TEACHER?

A teacher must be a communicator. Knowing your subject isn't enough; you must have the gift of making that subject lively and real to your students. Regardless of how accomplished you are in your field, unless you can communicate both facts and enthusiasm to your students, your efforts will be wasted.

Patience, too, is a vital ingredient in successful teaching. Since you know your subject well, the basics seem simple enough to you. But your students don't have that advantage.

The subject is new and strange to them. You'll have to remember how confused you felt when you first began learning the subject.

Patience is also necessary with the student who is eager but inept. Sometimes you may be confronted with a pupil who has enthusiasm and perhaps even understands the principles of what you are teaching, yet he lacks coordination or ability to accomplish the task on a practical level. For instance, I once took a ceramics course. Although my mind understood the delicacy of unfired greenware, my hands didn't seem to get the message. I was eager to learn—in fact, I was too eager. After breaking several pieces of greenware, I finally learned to be careful, but the patience of my teacher must have been sorely tried during the time it took me to learn to be careful.

WHAT CAN I TEACH?

Most people who think of teaching immediately think of teaching school subjects to children. Although this idea is certainly a possibility, it's not the only one. Any art, craft, or skill which you do reasonably well is a potential subject for a course you can teach to others. You need not have had professional training nor do you need any teacher certification degree. You can teach the basics of your subject and then refer "graduating" students to other sources if they desire further training which you are not qualified to give.

Crafts are not the only suitable subjects for teaching. When I ran a home sewing business I was frequently approached by desperate mothers who begged for sewing classes. I have never known anyone who actually conducted sewing classes on a one-to-one basis, but it seems there is a demand for such a class.

People also like to learn how to do things which will save them money. We are a nation of do-it-yourselfers, and the homeworker who can teach a money-saving skill will find a ready audience. Potential students would like to learn to grow a garden, to type, to repair their own cars, and to cook. In my community all of these skills are currently being taught by enterprising individuals who have learned to capitalize on the do-it-yourself mood.

HOW CAN I TEACH?

The first obstacle to teaching is that few women have extra space in their homes to accommodate a classroom. This need not be an obstacle. There's also a demand for teaching on a one-to-one basis. If you have room for yourself and one more person, you can find the space for conducting a class.

There's no rule that says all classes must be conducted inside your home. If you have a garage or a patio, perhaps you can conduct classes in these areas during the warmer months of the year. You might even confiscate the metal storage building in the backyard for your teaching purposes. Some ladies in my community use a little backyard storage barn for their classes in quilting techniques. Another woman I know has a kiln in her basement, and students work at a table sandwiched in between her family's storage spaces.

HOW MUCH SHALL I CHARGE?

A suitable charge for your teaching skills will be based on several factors. Will your knowledge be the only thing you are selling? If so, then teaching is your sole source of income and the price you charge should reflect this fact. Will you sell supplies as well? If you will be teaching macramé or ceramics, and will also be selling craft materials to your students, you can afford to offer lessons at a much lower price. In fact, most craft teachers find it more profitable to charge nothing at all, or else a nominal fee. The real profit comes from selling raw materials to the students.

The ceramics instructor I previously mentioned has her own kiln and an abundance of students for her twice-weekly classes. Yet, she accepts her students free of charge. What does she get out of her generosity? First of all, she owns most of the molds for the ceramic pieces her students most frequently request. Making her own greenware means an increased profit for her since there's little expense involved in the casting. Most of the objects her students create come from her own stock. The paint is bought from a wholesaler and is sold to the students at retail prices. Then the firing process brings in additional money. The usual formula for kiln firing is to charge half the price of the greenware for the service of firing it. Thus a piece of greenware which a student bought for $5.00 would cost the student an extra $2.50 for firing.

Whenever a teacher is involved in teaching something on a one-to-one basis, the fee she charges will have to be sufficient to offset her time. Consequently, even if no outside materials are used, the teacher will need to charge a higher rate for the one-to-one teaching than she would for a classroom situation. If twenty people are in an hour long class, a fee of a dollar per person will yield a tidy profit for the teacher, but if only one person is in the class, obviously the fee will have to be much higher. The teacher should clear at least the minimum hourly wage for her effort. If she can't make at least the minimum hourly wage she should consider changing her approach.

THE PROBLEMS OF TEACHING

Along with every means of making money with a home career there comes a certain amount of problems. Teaching is no exception. What can you expect if you decide to teach?

If your students are children and your subject is one not dear to their hearts, you may encounter discipline problems. The best solution is to never allow disruption to start in the first place. The teacher must establish in the beginning that she is in charge of the situation and that order must be maintained. It's best to start off being somewhat strict as it's easier to decrease strictness than it is to start off lenient and then try to get stricter. (The principal of my daughter's school jokingly tells parents that he forbids his teachers to smile until after Thanksgiving. Of course, he's teasing, but the point he's making is that it's better to start off with firmness.)

Children are accustomed to being students and usually adapt fairly well to classroom situations. Unless the student involved is a real troublemaker, most disruptions can be successfully dealt with as long as the teacher makes it clear that she is the one in charge.

Perhaps an even greater problem is maintaining discipline in a class filled with adults. "Discipline" may seem like a strange word to be applied to adults, but many teachers have found uncooperative adults to be a real problem in a classroom.

At one time my husband decided to take a class at a local college. He was quite interested in the subject and felt that the tuition money was well spent. However, after attending a few sessions, he quit in disgust. Some of the members of the class constantly distracted the teacher with conversation on other subjects. There was so much diversion that the real subject of the class was never covered. Lack of classroom discipline does not gain any teacher repeat business.

How can you keep a similar disaster from occurring in your classes? One of my instructors at the recreation center's exercise classes comes to mind. She was friendly, competent, and thoroughly interested in her subject and her students. Yet, in spite of her friendly before- and after-class banter, it was obvious to all of us that she was fully in charge of the class and the curriculum. Frequently, some member of the class would try to talk her out of having us do some particularly difficult exercise or would try to "con" her into letting us get by with a lesser number of strenuous exercises. She handled these suggestions by immediately launching vigorously into the exercise she had announced. We soon learned that she was open to suggestions before and after class but during class she was fully in charge.

Another problem, even with teaching adults, is that occasionally you may encounter a student who is in the class against her will. Strange as it may seem, some adults find themselves "tagging along" to courses they are not at all interested in. Perhaps a husband wants to take your course and insists that his wife come along to keep him company. And sometimes people will enroll in a course, not because they care about it, but merely to get out of the house one night a week. Students who are enrolled without any real interest can be virtually impossible to reach. Their minds wander, and they may even resent your efforts to get them into the classroom action.

Often people who are taking a course have no aptitude for the subject they are tackling even if they are enthusiastic. A lack of ability does not always indicate a lack of enthusiasm.

Betty James, a teacher of rosemaling, enjoys telling about an elderly lady who took to rosemaling with a passion. Unfortunately, this grandmotherly student had more enthusiasm than talent. But Betty is an excellent teacher and in a perceptive way found a means of dealing with the problem. She chose simple designs for her shaky-handed protégé, and instead of pointing out shortcomings, Betty complimented things such as color choice or appropriateness of design. The student had an enjoyable time, and although she'll never be a professional in decorative painting, she will find immense pleasure in her hobby because she was fortunate enough to have an understanding teacher.

WHAT ARE THE DISADVANTAGES OF BEING A TEACHER?

Most of the other problems of teaching, such as discipline, lack of interest, or even ineptitude can be dealt with by the teacher who combines patience, enthusiasm, and an interest in people. However, there are other teaching problems which are not as easily handled.

The greatest obstacle to successful teaching is the lack of flexibility in time scheduling. With most other home businesses you can set your own hours. If you are creating a product you do so at your own convenience. Teaching doesn't work that way. You must schedule classes at the time most convenient for your students. Unfortunately, this may mean you'll be holding classes after school hours or after work hours—the very times when you most want to be with your own family.

Another problem is that once you've set a specific time for classes, you are committed to that schedule. Consequently, you'll find yourself teaching when you don't feel well, or when you'd rather be outdoors playing tennis, or when the rest of your family is going out for ice cream.

Teaching demands your wholehearted concentration during school hours. If you were creating a product or performing a service you could let your mind wander, or you might even simultaneously be able to carry on a conversation, watch television, or mind the children. Teaching does not offer this advantage because teaching demands your complete attention. Even if you're tired or have a headache, your students are expecting your best. To a certain extent, being a teacher calls for acting ability, too. While you might be able to yawn occasionally while you baby-sit, or sew, or paint, you don't have that freedom if you teach. Even when you don't feel your best, you must be able to communicate enthusiasm to your students.

Service
Jobs

Perhaps you feel as though you are all thumbs and could never succeed in creating a salable product. And perhaps either your temperament or circumstances make teaching out of the question for you. Consequently, you've just about given up hope of finding a suitable home occupation. In spite of these problems, there *is* something you can do. Have you considered the possibility of performing a moneymaking service?

WHAT IS A SERVICE JOB?

A service job differs from other classifications in that it creates no product, nor imparts any knowledge to the customer. Instead, the service offers the customer a needed help which she cannot or will not provide for herself. The customer might seek your help because she lacks ability or time to do the task. In other cases, she may prefer to let you do the job, not because it is time consuming or difficult, but because she finds it personally distasteful to do the job for herself. This does not mean that the job is repulsive, merely that it is not particularly interesting to her. Such service jobs as ironing, dog-walking, or sewing might seem dull to your customer and yet, if those are your areas of interest, you won't find the job boring at all.

HOW DO I CHOOSE A SERVICE JOB?

The selection of a service job is a matter of personal taste. The choice is made according to your own individuality and circumstances. The service should, however, be one you enjoy when you do it for yourself and should also be one which people will be willing to pay to have performed. A good indication of what services can be performed for profit can be found by talking with your friends. Ask them what tasks they dislike or find little time to do. Even if they never use your service, the ideas you glean may show you what sort of chores people are interested in avoiding. Then work out the details of your service job in accordance with your own likes and dislikes. For instance, if you hate to do your own ironing, don't make the mistake of agreeing to iron for anyone else. Regardless of how profitable a service may be, if you don't enjoy it, leave it alone.

HOW DO I GET STARTED?

Some service jobs will naturally require equipment, so if your chosen profession does require an investment, get the necessary tools first, whether they be typewriter, ironing board, or sewing machine. After this, you are ready to start organizing your work area in preparation for opening your doors to business.

A vital step in any service job is to first be certain you know how to do the job. While this might seem elementary, it's surprising how many people try to start work without first being certain of their own capabilities. If you start receiving customers before you're adequately skilled, you'll only hurt your chances for business in the future.

Advertising is crucial to service jobs because you are creating no easily seen product—a disadvantage a craftsman does not have. Unless you are doing some sort of service which no one has thought of before, you won't be likely to attract free publicity the way craftspeople do. The local radio station simply won't interview a lady who baby-sits for extra dollars, nor will the local paper do an in-depth profile of the neighborhood's best typist. (Your only chance at fame is to baby-sit someone like the president's grandchild or to type for someone like Queen Elizabeth—both tasks are easier said than done.) When it comes to publicity for service jobs you're strictly on your own.

A well-worded newspaper ad run in several consecutive editions will start you on your way. If you plan a service which is specialized and can be conducted through the mail, you might also find it profitable to advertise in related publications. A manuscript typist should consider an ad in *Writer's Digest*. An owner of a doll repair service would be investing dollars wisely in an ad in *National Doll World*.

Business cards are also helpful if you are running a service business. As with advertising, make sure you use your business cards in the most productive manner possible. If you plan to take in ironing, pass out cards to people who are coming out of the laundromat. If you want to groom poodles position yourself near the veterinarian's office. Give your cards to friends and ask them to hand one to anyone who asks if they know someone who does your particular speciality.

WHAT ABOUT CUSTOMERS?

If you choose a service job do so with the realization that you must deal with people. Relatively few services can be done without face-to-face contact with your customers. (Mail order services are the exception, but even mail order involves contact although it's not on a face-to-face basis.) If you are especially shy you might prefer a service job which can be done for the same customers over and over so that you have a chance to get to know your customers and won't be continually facing strangers.

One of the disadvantages of a service job is that you are quite frequently performing your service on an object which the customer already owns. Whether the object be his poodle, which needs grooming, or his suit which needs the trouser legs hemmed, you are working on something that does not belong to you. While an accident with your own handmade pottery might not be so traumatic, nipping the ear of someone's show dog or cutting too much fabric off someone's expensive new suit could be disastrous. Customers might be nervous about having you work on their prized possessions. Accordingly, don't be too intimidated if they ask for references or if they require you to show work you have done.

THE DISADVANTAGES OF SERVICE JOBS

The main disadvantage of service jobs is the monotony. Of course, not all tasks will be monotonous, but many are. If you are creating a product, often you can vary the design or the ingredients in order to relieve your boredom with sameness. Service jobs don't offer that advantage. There aren't many ways to vary a typed page or a prepared income tax form. However, the disadvantage of sameness is more than amply offset by the diversity in customers. The work you do for each customer may be identical but the reactions will be determined by the customers' individual personality traits. Dealing with customers may occasionally try your patience, but it's certainly never dull!

Another disadvantage is that some service jobs tend to tie you down. If you perform a service where the customer must bring something to you and then return to pick it up again, you are somewhat limited by his coming and going. While the craftswoman sets her own hours and the teacher sets consistent hours, the owner of a service business has less flexibility. You have to let the customer come at a time convenient for him and the time won't always be the same. The best you can do is let customers know what hours you are not available, such as your dinner hour, and hope they will not intrude at those times. It's convenient to have them call before they come, but most won't bother to do that. They want to "drop in" on you just as they "drop in" at a store.

IDEAS FOR SERVICE JOBS

Service jobs offer more variations than do the other two categories. For this reason, I'll mention a few possibilities just to get you started thinking.

photo restoring
answering service

baby-sitting
bookkeeping
preparing income tax returns
forwarding mail
typing
composing for printers
dog grooming
hair care
quilting
sewing
antique restoring
shopping for others
free-lance research
caring for plants for vacationers
pet-sitting
addressing Christmas cards for business firms
being a notary public
being a locksmith
repairing small appliances or clocks
repairing old dolls
doing special cleaning chores such as polishing silver
doing laundry
ironing
washing and waxing cars

The Mother Earth News is a bi-monthly publication which will give you innumerable ideas for other home service businesses. *The Mother Earth News* contains detailed how-to information, written not by theorizing "experts," but by ordinary people who have actually successfully done the jobs which they are writing about. For subscription rates write to:

The Mother Earth News
P.O. Box 70
Hendersonville, NC 28739

The
Older
Woman

When careers as homeworkers are mentioned, many people immediately think about young wives and mothers struggling to make ends meet and anxiously trying to earn a few extra dollars to help balance the budget. However, mothers of preschoolers aren't the only homemakers who find a home business enjoyable and profitable.

WHY WOULD AN OLDER WOMAN NEED A CAREER AT HOME?

One of the prime motivations for any woman's home business is the need for personal fulfillment. Regardless of your age, you always need something to work for and to look forward to. Unfortunately, many people spend their lives eagerly looking forward to retirement only to discover that idleness breeds boredom. Still others face an even worse dilemma. They plan an activity filled retirement only to find lifelong plans curtailed by bad health or inflation's pinch on retirement's fixed income.

Whatever their retirement situations may be, many older women are discovering that a home career is the perfect solution to boredom and to a cash shortage. While younger women must schedule business activities during school hours or during the baby's naptime, the older woman has no such restrictions. Retirement years bring the freedom to schedule business along relaxed time lines. Retired people can rise when they wish, eat when they wish, and, unless the home occupation is vital to the budget, they can work when they wish. An added advantage is the enjoyable togetherness a home career can offer to retired couples. Work can become more enjoyable when shared with a life partner. Instead of the friction and squabbles inherent in some retired couples' relationships, the retired couple who works as a team may find themselves having the time of their lives.

PROBLEMS OF THE OVER-SIXTY SET

What can you as a "retired" homemaker expect if you begin a career after sixty? Like all other phases of the homemaker's life, this period offers some difficulties to the enterprising would-be businesswoman. However, the problems are not greater than the problems faced by younger women, they are simply different.

1. Are you physically able to handle a new career? While many older women enjoy good health, many are plagued by ailments which would interfere with certain careers. However, unless the ailment is such that merely managing to breathe is a major triumph, a homemaker who is willing to be flexible about her choice can likely find some sort of work which she can do. Many successful homeworkers do not enjoy perfect health, yet they find a way to work around their problems. I once talked to a woman whose legs are crippled by polio. Because of her handicap, she is unable to work at a traditional job. However, she has a good income derived from the sale of a very original craft. She works a few local craft shows each year, but the bulk of her income comes from selling to wholesalers.

Dorothy Chenoweth is another example of a woman who has overcome a physical problem in order to be a successful businesswoman. Dorothy, who creates beautiful jewelry from quail eggs, has arthritis in her hands. Although Dorothy is unable to hold a pair of scissors in the usual manner, she has devised a method of cutting out tiny designs to be applied to the eggs. No one who looks at the exquisite finished jewelry would ever suspect that Dorothy used any method other than the orthodox one.

2. How does your husband feel about the career? The woman over sixty faces husband problems quite unlike the problems faced by younger homeworkers. Men who were raised to believe the head of the household has the sole responsibility for providing the living do not suddenly change their philosophy after their sixtieth birthday. A man who has spent most of his life providing monetarily for his family may not take kindly to his wife's sudden interest in making money. The problem is not cruelty, nor jealousy, but rather the set of values which have governed the husband's life. The wise wife will work gently with her husband to help him change his attitude. The ideal situation, of course, is one where both partners can find equal participation in the home business project. But if the new career is something totally feminine-seeming to the husband, he may still refuse to participate. Yet even such things as knitting and sewing can be the basis for a partnership if the couple is willing to work out a solution.

Some neighbors of mine—a couple in their late sixties—found a way to work together on a moneymaking business. First, the wife crochets an intricate, old-fashioned doily. Then the husband takes over. Carefully, he prepares a special starch, and, using bottles to shape the doily's ruffles, he coaxes the creation into its proper shape. Then the doily is carefully placed in a cardboard box to preserve its starched perfection. Later the husband puts aside his role as craftsman and instead becomes the salesman.

3. Will your children cooperate? While it seems logical that a mother with toddlers would have problems running a home business, it seems strange that a grandmother would find her moneymaking efforts thwarted by grown-up offspring. Yet, sadly this is true in many cases. Adult offspring sometimes forget that parents are adults, too, and deserve the right to make their own decisions. How does the older woman tactfully deal with this? Each case will be different, but a grandmother with business plans must find a way to diplomatically inform her children that she has a life of her own. Watching television and baby-sitting grandchildren is not enough mental stimulation to be the total of any woman's retirement years. While children mean well in advising parents to "take it easy," each person must do what is right for herself, regardless of others' well-meaning advice.

4. Do you need the money? It's a sad fact of life that many retired couples exist on meager incomes. Many couples carefully plan for retirement only to discover that inflation has destroyed their hopes and dreams. For some "retired" women, a home business is not just an entertainment, nor the source of pin money, but a vital ingredient in keeping groceries on the table. To add to the problem, a person receiving social security payments is not allowed to make much money in addition to the payments. If a homeworker has a business that is reasonably successful, she may run the risk of losing her social security check. There's a way to get around that problem, too.

The retiree might consider bartering some of her services instead of receiving cash. Bartering seems somewhat old-fashioned, but it's still a good way to get what you need. For instance, at one time I baby-sat for a friend's baby. Her husband was a butcher, so instead of getting paid in cash, I requested payment in meat. At that time—1968—baby sitters were being paid about fifteen dollars per week. Yet, my first week's efforts brought me roasts and New York strip steaks. At 1968 prices, I had earned the equivalent of at least thirty dollars worth of meat.

At other times I have exchanged my sewing skills for products and services I needed. I made a pair of slacks for a beautician in exchange for her giving me a haircut. A custom-made dress for a jewelry-maker brought me some lovely pieces of jewelry which I used as Christmas gifts that year.

Bartering *does* work, and it can at the same time help you avoid being penalized on the social security payments you receive. If you want more ideas about bartering, check at your newsstand for *The Mother Earth News*. There is a column in each issue which tells about successful swaps. Some of the ideas mentioned might stimulate your own thinking on the subject. Pending IRS regulations may make it necessary to declare the value of bartered service on income tax returns. You may wish to investigate this ruling before engaging in a lot of bartering.

5. Do you need training? Unlike the young married woman, the older woman may be years away from her last classroom experience. What can you do when you've forgotten so much or

67

are so out of practice that pursuing the profession you were trained for is totally out of the question? Go back to school! Many people in their sixties are unaware of the plethora of educational opportunities which abound for them. Not only do retirees benefit from being able to take classes at any time they choose, they also benefit from being able to take some classes free. Colleges often offer adult education classes for nominal fees to anyone, and if your neighborhood is like mine, the classes may be free to retirees. The junior college near my home offers non-credit courses in everything from creative writing and photography to mechanics or dog training. Some high schools also offer training at night school. I once took a real estate course which lasted for ten weeks and cost five dollars. For a retiree, with prices like that the cost of a refresher course in your chosen field is no stumbling block.

6. Are you too old to start something new? Maybe you *are* too old if you think you are! Some people are already old by the time they reach their twenty-fifth birthday while other people carry young minds around in octogenarian bodies.

Grandma Moses didn't think she was too old to start a new career the year she had her seventy-sixth birthday and took up oil painting. She was an active needleworker and previously had kept herself busy with embroidery. Yet when stiff fingers forced her to give up needlework, she began a new career and painted for twenty-six years after that! Grandma Moses wasn't old even when she had her seventy-sixth birthday.

Now, are *you* too old?

BUT WHAT CAN I DO?

Like your younger friends, you may be perplexed over what actual opportunities are available for you. Just like any other homemaker, you must sit down and honestly assess your own personal preferences, motivation, available time, and financial goals. However, as an older woman, you have some valuable extra points in your favor. Experience and maturity are priceless assets, so in tallying up your good points don't sell yourself short. Any woman who has successfully raised her children, has managed a home for forty years, and has kept a husband happy certainly has her hardest chores behind her. A little thing like a new career certainly shouldn't faze a woman with that kind of track record!

Advertising and Publicity

Perhaps you are the greatest teacher in the world, or have the world's most salable craft, or even know how to do some essential service no one else can do. But you will never get money for what you do unless people *know* about it, and that's where advertising enters the home business picture.

FREE ADVERTISING

Of course, the most desirable advertising is the kind you get free. But unless you are in an unusual occupation or your father owns the local paper, free advertising is hard to obtain. Yet even if your advertising budget is zero and your father doesn't own the newspaper, you can use a totally free form of advertising—word of mouth. Word of mouth takes a while and presents one problem: you can't get customers until you advertise and you can't get word of mouth advertising until you have customers. How do you solve a seemingly unsolvable dilemma? Try "buying" some word of mouth advertising.

When I first started a home sewing business, as might be expected, I had no prospective customers. Nevertheless, I did have an asset equally valuable to an enterprising businesswoman—I had friends. Therefore, after telling practically everyone I knew of my intentions to start a home sewing business, I got down to specifics. Some of my friends were in positions where word of mouth would be particularly effective. Consequently, I approached a few likely subjects with a deal they couldn't refuse: I would sew one garment for them at half price for each new customer they brought to me. Now, admittedly, this plan is a form of paid advertising, but a relatively painless one for a beginning homeworker with no advertising budget. I priced my work high enough to assure that even though I sold a few garments at half price, I made something for my efforts. At the same time, I had enough confidence in my sewing ability to feel that after someone had one of my custom-made garments, she would be back for more. My idea worked so well that I actually had to make only two half-priced items. Word spread by customers carried the business from there.

Another way of "buying" free advertising is through labeling your work. At one time, I made all the model garments used by a local fabric store. Since most shoppers find inspecting the model garments irresistible, I decided to put their curiosity to good use. Each outfit I made was as nearly perfect as I could make it. Then I attached a label which stated, "Made especially for you by Edith Kilgo." These labels cost three dollars per hundred and quickly paid for themselves by bringing in all the new customers I could handle. The store maintained a list of neighborhood seamstresses for the benefit of nonsewing customers. Customers didn't know the quality of those other seamstresses' work, but my work was readily available for inspection, and that noticeable label gave me a definite advantage over my competitors.

Those labels brought me free advertising in another way, too. I had noticed that my more style-conscious patrons felt it an honor to wear custom-made clothing. Consequently, I began sewing my label into the garments I made for them. They loved it. One lady proudly told me she attended a social function and deliberately placed her jacket over her chair in such a manner as to make the label obvious! Remember, your name can be your advertisement, too. Proudly label your work, regardless of whether your product is a ceramic pot or a handwoven shawl.

NEWSPAPER ADVERTISING

More home businesses advertise in the newspaper than any other place. The cost of a newspaper ad is small, but the ads are seen by many potential customers. In spite of the popularity of newspaper advertising, it's amazing how many people don't know the most effective ways of writing and placing ads.

If you live in a suburb of a large city, you'll have several options when it comes to choosing a newspaper for advertising purposes. Generally, there's a sophisticated, widely distributed, big city newspaper which carries all the national and international news. Frequently, the classified advertising section in this paper is the thickest portion of the paper. Then there's usually a daily or weekly suburban paper. While this newspaper may cover to a limited degree world news, at least two-thirds of it is devoted to local issues. In addition to this newspaper, many communities have a free paper which is usually provided once a week or twice a month through the mail. These newspapers concentrate exclusively on local people and events. At least half the paper consists of local sports events or social affairs. An increasingly popular suburban newspaper is the "shopper." This is a free paper that is thrown into your front yard once a week. Basically, the shopper contains local advertising and "happy news"—stories about golden wedding anniversaries or articles on how to plant a garden. With so many choices, how can you place your ad in the paper that will bring you the most business?

The best way to choose is to compare cost versus effectiveness. While the big city daily newspaper may charge you twenty dollars or more for one ad, frequently the shoppers will run a ten-word ad for as little as one dollar. The local dailies usually charge more—rates of perhaps one-fourth as much as those charged by the big city daily newspaper. Thus, you have a choice. For twenty dollars you can get one ad in the metropolitan paper, or four ads in the local daily paper, or twenty weekly ads in the free papers. Of course, the number of times the ad appears is not the only consideration. Circulation figures count, too. The metropolitan paper may be read by a million or more subscribers, while the local papers may be read by only ten thousand. Yet, circulation figures can deceive you, too. Do you know anyone who regularly reads *all* the classified ads in the big paper? I don't, and I imagine you don't either. However, a large percentage of readers frequently check out the local dailies and perhaps an even larger percentage read practically every ad in the free papers. The reason: the ads are entertainment. Since they cost so little all sorts of goods and services are advertised there.

Which newspaper will work best for your needs? To find out give the least expensive ads a trial run, and gauge your effectiveness by calculating how much business is generated for each advertising dollar you spend. One inquiry from a one dollar ad is actually more profitable than is a similar ad which draws five responses but costs you twenty dollars to run.

In most cases, newspaper ads are paid for by the word. However, this system can involve varying rates, depending on the size type you want used for the ad. Newspapers charge higher rates for larger type. Type is classified by points. The larger the point type you choose, the higher your cost will be. You can also mix type sizes. A combination of regular size type with a slightly larger, bolder-faced type is a good attention getter.

The wording of the ad is crucial to its success. Don't use unfamiliar words or abbreviations or leave the reader with any doubt about what you are offering for sale. Be as concise as possible for the sake of the price-per-word fee, but do put all the necessary facts into the ad. The ad for my home sewing business was worded:

> Custom dressmaking and alterations. Fast service. Reasonable rates. Edith Kilgo. 465-9899.

The ad told exactly what service was being offered and at the same time let the prospective customer know I was understanding about emergencies and budgets. Since mine was the type of service which had no set fee but was based on the amount of time and effort in each garment, I refrained from mentioning any prices.

Most people prefer to start a telephone conversation with a stranger by at least knowing a name. It's awkward to call someone and have to say, "Are you the lady that does dressmaking?" Using your name in the ad gives you another benefit, too. Some of your acquaintances may not have known about your business, but after they see your name in the paper they'll mention it to others even if they never use your product or service themselves.

MAGAZINE ADVERTISING

Magazine advertising is expensive and worthwhile only if properly placed. Some of the major magazines have shopper's sections or classifieds. These ads resemble the classified section of your newspaper, but even the "little ads" may be expensive if the magazine you have in mind is a well-known one with a million-plus circulation.

Since you'll be paying three to four dollars *per word,* it becomes absolutely vital to word your ad as clearly and succinctly as possible. Not only will you have the high cost per word to contend with, you may also discover that the magazine you've chosen is not interested in running one-time ads. Some publications will require you to purchase a three-month block of advertising as the minimum they'll accept. If this is the case, you'll want to be certain before you commit yourself to the expense that you've chosen the right publication, the right time of year, and the right product or service.

Most magazines have a deadline of thirty to sixty days prior to publication for receiving advertising copy. However, this can be misleading. Let's suppose you want to advertise in the April issue of your chosen periodical. Since the April issue will be on the newsstands around mid-March, the magazine staff must have the material ready for the printer from three to six months before the date on the cover. This means the material for the April issue may be compiled as early as November. Since the deadline for advertising copy is thirty to sixty days prior to that, you may well have to have your April ad ready and at the editorial office as early as September!

If you decide to invest in more costly advertising, the larger display ads may fill your needs. If you do use this type of advertising, you'll need good quality black and white photographs. Readers are much more likely to buy items and services which are pictured rather than merely described. Since the display ads are quite expensive—often in the hundreds of dollars for a fraction of a page—you'll need the most effective ad you can devise. If you're willing to invest so much money in advertising, perhaps it would be advisable to invest a bit more and have your ad prepared by a professional ad writer.

If you feel that advertising in magazines is the best route for you, but you don't have the necessary funds, there is a way to obtain display advertising without investing any money. Some magazines are receptive to the idea of "per inquiry" ads. This means that you pay nothing for the ad, but for each order you receive as a result of the ad, you'll pay the magazine a fee. In order for this to appeal to the publisher, you must offer some sort of basis on which to convince him of your product's enthusiastic reception by his readers. For example, if you've devised a revolutionary new knitting needle, you wouldn't offer it to *Popular Mechanics*. Instead, you'd go to the library, find magazines which offer knitting instructions and feature ads for knitting supplies. Then, after looking through perhaps a year of back issues, you'd determine which ads were continually run month after month. If one of the products was some sort of knitting needle, you'd have found an acceptable means of approaching the publisher with your per-inquiry idea. Point out to him that your competitor is successfully month after month selling enough to compensate for the high-priced ad and that since your product is innovative and of a high quality, it is logical to assume you'll do well also. If the ad rate is five hundred dollars and you offer to pay two dollars per inquiry, the publisher will have to receive 250 inquiries just to make his ad rate. If, however, you can offer him five dollars per inquiry and can provide some basis for the belief that your ad will generate as many as one thousand inquiries, the publisher might be willing to go along with your plan. Not all magazines are receptive to the per inquiry approach, but it doesn't hurt to try.

SIGNS

A sign at your door or in your yard may boost income, but before you invest money in having a sign painted it's wise to check on zoning restrictions regarding signs. Your neighbors might not be as thrilled over your favorite sign painter's work of art as you are. Therefore, if you put up a sign without checking the regulations first, you might be wasting your money.

Your neighbors might justly have reason to complain if you install a blinking neon sign or anything else that might destroy the neighborhood's residential look.

If you are unable to advertise with a worded sign consider using pictures. When I had a home sewing business I wanted to put up a discreet little sign stating, "Dressmaking and Alterations," but the city ordinances ruled out that possibility. However, a very helpful lady at city hall suggested a clever alternative.

"Why don't you have a sign painted with no words," she said. "You could use a picture of a spool of thread and a pair of scissors. People would understand the meaning of the sign, but you wouldn't be breaking the law. After all, it is perfectly legal to decorate your house or yard with paintings if you choose to do so."

Pictures do get the message across to potential customers. There was a time when hardly anyone could read and *all* advertising was done with pictorial signs or other symbols of the trade—that's how the barber pole and the pawn shop balls came to be associated with those two businesses.

An alternative method of advertisement in areas where yard signs are prohibited is the increasingly popular magnetic sign. These magnetic name plates are designed to adhere to the side of a car. To advertise in this manner, you simply park your car in the driveway so the sign is easily visible to passers-by.

THE TELEPHONE DIRECTORY

You may be wondering if it's worthwhile to have your business listed in the yellow pages of the telephone book. The listing may indeed help you, but remember that having your business listed in this manner changes your telephone classification from personal use to business use. This means your rates will nearly double. You'll need to weigh the advantages of the listing in order to determine if the chance at increased income will justify the increased cost of overhead.

If you do go to a business listing, you'll most likely need a separate phone for family use. You can't expect customers to call if your teen-ager stays on the phone for hours at a time. And since you will be paying to have a business listing, you will want the maximum advantage from it.

Remember, too, that a business phone is a legitimate tax deduction, while a home phone, even when used occasionally for business purposes, is not. (Business related long distance charges are always deductible, too, regardless of whether or not you have a business listing.)

Having a business phone gets your business listed in the yellow pages, but gives you no extra advertising. If you want more than just a name, address, and phone number shown, you must pay extra. A listing in the yellow pages may prove helpful if you perform the sort of service which customers will need infrequently. Any sort of work that can be done over and over will generate enough repeat customers to keep you in business without your going to the expense of having a yellow page listing. With my sewing business, I originally considered a yellow page ad, but later I was glad I had not followed my original inclination. After the first three months of business, I had so many steady, repeat customers that I couldn't accept any new ones.

PUBLICITY

Publicity is free advertising such as newspaper or magazine articles or radio or television interviews. It can be wonderful, *if* the publicist spells your name right and gets the story straight. However, since he is doing it gratis, you might not have much control over the final results.

A frequently overlooked source of publicity is the local paper—not the ads, but the actual paper. Large city newspapers may not express much interest in your "news," but usually somewhere in every city there is a little weekly newspaper hungry for "people news." Call the editor and you may soon find yourself opening the door for a reporter and photographer. If the editor is polite, but declines to send someone to interview you, ask him if he will run a news release. A news release is a brief publicity statement worded to masquerade as regular news. Most local editors will extend this courtesy to you and your fledgling business even if they have no interest in what you had hoped for—a full-length, in-depth profile. Women's clubs, historical societies, and even shopping centers use this kind of free publicity all the time.

To prepare your news release, type a concise paragraph giving all the pertinent facts. If possible, include a glossy 8″ × 10″ photograph. (A story with a photograph included is more likely to get a prominent position on the page.) However, the pictures *must* be of good quality, *must* be black and white, and should be an 8″ × 10″ or at least a 5″ × 7″. When the film is processed, emphasize that it must be printed on glossy paper. Other kinds of paper do not print well on newsprint pages. If you can't get some family member to take an appropriate picture, try asking at the camera store, local college, or recreation center for some talented amateur who might be willing to take the photograph for you. A professional photographer will charge more than the publicity is likely to be worth, but a hobbyist might well work for you much cheaper. Don't have the photograph developed at the corner drugstore either. Look in the yellow pages for a custom processing lab. The cost will be greater but the quality will be worth it. Newspapers are not printed on high quality paper, so in order for a photograph to reproduce well it must have good contrast between the black and white elements.

When you present your news release, have it typed as neatly as possible and include your name, address, and phone number on the typed sheet and the photograph. If you expect to have the photograph returned, make a notation of that fact and include a stamped, self-addressed envelope for its return. On the material write "for immediate release."

If you don't get stage fright, and if you can think fast under pressure, getting yourself booked on either a local radio or television show is a wonderful source of publicity. Most cities have the type of radio programs where a guest is interviewed by an announcer who then lets listeners call in to ask questions of the guest. Listen to a few weeks of the program you are considering and then call the station's program director. These program directors need hundreds of guests each year so if you are reasonably intelligent and are able to talk animatedly about your work, you will likely get a chance to be a guest. Television shows are a bit harder to get into. Call for an appointment to meet with the program director. If he is interested enough to agree to meet you, you will need to be not only articulate, but neat and nicely dressed. (I said "neat," not beautiful, and "nicely dressed," not expensively dressed.)

Another source of free publicity is magazines. While most of the smaller magazines don't have the staff or money to send someone across the country to interview you, there is a way to circumvent that problem. If there is a writer's club in your community, locate it and see if some of the aspiring writers would like to do a manuscript about your work. If you can't locate a writer's club, you might also consult the night school teacher who teaches creative writing at the local college. Maybe you will be so charming that he will assign your story to the whole class and let you pick the best manuscript to send off! At any rate, don't pay for this service. Have it clearly understood that *if* the writer can get the manuscript published, he gets all the magazine paycheck—even though you helped a lot. Magazine publicity is actually not too helpful as far as creating actual sales. It is, however, invaluable as a selling point in showing a craft fair promoter how well-known you are. Publicity also opens the door to many of the more exclusive shops and galleries.

If all attempts at free advertising fail, a little priming of the advertising pump may be necessary. Some very small, one-man publications may react more favorably to your attempt at publicity if you at first advertise for a few months in their classified section. After the editor gets to know you, perhaps he or she will be more interested in printing a story about your work. Never underestimate the value of having an article in even a magazine that is a shoe-string operation with a limited circulation. Most writers, myself included, make a regular practice of reading all sorts of magazines in their search for potential article ideas. Even if you think a picture story in *Hog Caller's Weekly Bulletin* won't help you, don't turn away your chance at free publicity. You never know who might read that article and where his reading it might lead.

THE PERSONAL TOUCH

Calling prospective customers on the telephone is another way of generating business without spending money on advertising. You can't call everybody in town, but selective telephoning may get you the clients you need.

Phone calls are generally effective only if you can predetermine that your audience will have an interest in your product, service, or teaching. For example, suppose you are planning to give Spanish lessons. A list of all the high school students who are having difficulties with this subject might well put you in business after you make a few phone calls. Selective phone calls would be fine, but a list of the entire student body would be more trouble than it's worth.

THE ETHICS OF ADVERTISING

Christian businesswomen have an obligation to conduct any advertising campaigns in the most honest and forthright manner possible. Therefore, each advertisement must say only what you mean and exactly what you mean. Some ads are misleading, not because the writer of the ad had fraud as her intent, but because the vagueness of the ad left too many possibilities for misinterpretation by the reader.

Some Christian homeworkers also wonder if it is right to use friends to generate business. As long as the friendship is not abused, there's no harm in selling to friends. The problem starts only when making dollars becomes overly important and the businesswoman has time only for "friends" who can advance her financial cause.

You Don't Have to Fight City Hall

Finally, everything is ready, and your doors are about to swing wide to accommodate the rush of customers. The house is clean, supper is simmering, the children are cooperating, and business will be booming in five minutes.

Wait! Have you taken care of your responsibilities at city hall?

As Christians, we must obey the law of the land. Even though your business is only a tiny one, and it doesn't take up much room or even make much money, it is still a business. Accordingly, legal requirements for business must be dealt with in compliance of the law. Don't panic. You won't need a course in double-entry bookkeeping or business law.

ZONING REQUIREMENTS

Have you checked the zoning restriction in your neighborhood? Zoning codes are in effect in most cities. These codes are used to consolidate each section of the city into areas restricted to one specific land use. All the stores are in one area, the manufacturers are in another, and the houses in yet another. You have the assurance that your house is surrounded only by other houses and doesn't have to be sandwiched between a drive-in movie and a fertilizer factory.

Fortunately most cities have fairly lenient rules regarding home businesses. The town fathers certainly have sense enough to know that many citizens are going to try to make extra money at home. These gentlemen have an eye on the ballot box so they don't want to alienate any potential voters. However, they have to consider both sides of the question. They want to keep you, a business proprietor, happy with them, but, at the same time, they must placate the neighbors.

Since the majority of home business proprietors never bother to comply with regulations, you likely will find that city hall is favorably impressed with your efforts at good citizenship and will gladly cooperate with you as much as possible.

You may be wondering why you must comply with the law when others don't. This goes back to the issue of Christian responsibilities. Even if the rest of the world ignores a law we have an obligation to uphold it. All it takes is one irate neighbor's complaint to city hall, and your home business, as well as your Christian testimony, is gone.

Usually zoning restrictions in residential areas will not stop you from conducting a home business as long as it does not interfere with your neighbor's rights. This means you can't allow your customers to block streets and driveways, nor can you erect signs which will lower your neighbors' property values. Basically, an application of common sense will help you determine what you can and cannot do. Just put yourself in your neighbor's shoes and ask yourself how you would feel if the situation were reversed.

BUSINESS LICENSES

The proprietor of a home business should always acquire a home business license or permit. Although many people disagree with me on this point, the fact remains—it is the law. Obtaining a business permit is neither a frightening nor expensive procedure. You simply go to city hall, spend five minutes filling out forms, part with a nominal amount of money (in my city it is fifteen dollars), and you have a business permit. The permit is good for one year and should be displayed in your work area so that customers can see it.

Although getting that business license does take a little bit of time, money, and effort, the principle behind the law is quite worthwhile. Picture what life in your community would be like if somebody decided to run a year-round flea market on the corner of your street. *Then* you would applaud city hall's method of licensing businesses! Besides, look on the bright side. Suppose a newcomer calls city hall and asks if there is anyone who does your particular specialty. Since you are recorded at city hall, the potential customer can be directed to you.

ADVERTISING RESTRICTIONS

While exploring the restrictions on home businesses, check into the matter of signs. In most residential areas advertising is not allowed at all. Other areas may allow you to have a small, discreet little sign as long as it does not make the neighborhood look garish. Whatever the situation, find out *first*. After paying twenty-five dollars to a sign painter, it's discouraging to discover your sign is prohibited. You may know of someone who has a beauty parlor in her home and flaunts a neon sign in the front yard. Certainly these things happen when either there are no zoning restrictions or the neighbors are too good-natured to complain.

COMPLYING WITH PARKING RESTRICTIONS

Parking restrictions should also be investigated before you begin receiving customers. On many streets, such as the curved one where I live, parking on the street is strictly prohibited. Unfortunately, there isn't always a "No Parking" sign to tell you this, so the only ways you can find out are by asking or by having a customer get a parking ticket. Since parking tickets are not really a fantastic way of attracting customers, you will find it simpler to ask before the problem arises. Then if there are restrictions, you can warn your customers in advance.

13

How to Get Along with Uncle Sam

The scariest part of starting a home business is learning to cope with all the legalities involved. You know you have to pay taxes, and you are sincere about wanting to do everything right, but where do you start?

IN THE BEGINNING

The best place to start is by getting someone you trust and who is knowledgeable on the subject of taxes, to fill out your first year's forms for you. No matter how many books you read on the subject, unless you really are a mathematician at heart, tax returns are going to be difficult for you. The returns for your first year of business will be the hardest ones to prepare, but if you have an accountant or a tax preparation firm help you, you will likely learn more than enough to offset the cost involved in having the work done for you.

Be certain to carry to your tax return preparer every scrap of paper which substantiates any deduction, no matter how small that deduction may be. Also, don't simply leave the material with the tax return preparer and return for it when he is finished. Instead, sit there with him and ask questions as he works. Even if you never intend to fill out the forms yourself, seeing the work done will give you a better perspective of what is needed in the matter of record keeping.

WHAT CAN I DEDUCT?

Of course, the object of having a business is to show a profit, but since expenses do occur, and since the Internal Revenue allows deductions for them, it is poor business to miss a single allowable deduction.

Some of the legal deductions are raw materials for the product you create, salaries paid to other employees, travel expenses, mileage, insurance, home office, business entertainment.

You can also deduct the cost of any fees paid to join professional organizations necessary to your trade or craft. Additionally, some specialized publications which are magazines or periodicals pertaining to your trade, are also allowable as deductions.

If your business occasionally takes you away from home, your motel bill and food bill are legitimate deductions, too. Just make certain you can positively prove the trip was for business and not pleasure because the Internal Revenue is strict about this. While making your trip, remember to record the miles you drive because you get a seventeen cent deduction for each mile. This mileage deduction applies also to any local traveling that you do. Even a trip around the block to deliver your product qualifies as business mileage.

One deduction that seems to always cause confusion is the home office deduction. Although this deduction is legally allowable, certain stipulations must be met. The portion of your home designated as an office must be used for that purpose only. Even the presence of a television set might lose the deduction for you if the Internal Revenue sends someone out to check. A home office *must* be for business use exclusively. (That is another disadvantage of running a business off the dining room table—you miss an important tax break.) You are entitled to deduct not only the rent for that room, but also you may deduct a portion of your home utility bills, too. For example, if you have a seven-room house, one-seventh of your yearly electric bill and one-seventh of your yearly heating bill are deductible. Long distance business phone calls are deductible, but your family telephone bill is not. (To get a telephone deduction you must have a phone used exclusively for business purposes.)

WHAT FORMS MUST I FILL OUT?

Form 1040 C. This form is entitled Profit (or Loss) from Business or Profession (Sole Proprietorship). This form is the one for listing all those deductions and for declaring any taxable profit which your business has shown. Predictable expenses, such as rent, salaries, etc., are listed on the form, and there are additional blanks for other allowable deductions.

Form 1040 SE. This is the form for paying your required self-employment tax. If your net income (the money you had left after all the deductions were subtracted) is as much as four hundred dollars a year, you must pay the self-employment tax. The rate for this tax is 8.1 percent, so you will want to be sure to take every allowable deduction in order to reduce the amount of taxes you will pay. (Caution: If you have allowable deductions and do *not* take them you can be penalized for that, too, because paying the self-employment tax on a larger income makes you eligible for greater social security benefits.)

Form 1040 ES. This is the form which is called the Estimated Tax Declaration. As a self-employed businesswoman, you will no longer pay taxes once a year, but you will be required to estimate your income for the coming year and pay your taxes four times a year in quarterly installments based on your estimation of what you will make during the coming year. Be sure to be as realistically accurate as possible in estimating your tax, because if your income is such that your yearly tax will exceed one hundred dollars, you *must* file Form 1040 ES or be penalized. Even though your estimation of your taxes is not correct, by filing Form 1040 ES, you can avoid the penalty. Then, if after filing your returns for the year, you discover that your estimate of taxes was too little the balance can be paid at that time. If your estimate of taxes exceeded your obligation, you will get a refund.

WHERE CAN I GET HELP?

A vital booklet for confused taxpayers is the Tax Guide for Small Businesses, available from the Internal Revenue Service. In it all your responsibilities, deductions, and filing information are explained in complete detail. If you live near an IRS office, you can call or stop by and employees there will answer your questions.

OTHER TAX CONSIDERATIONS

When you become a self-employed businesswoman, you also have another matter of taxes with which you must contend. If you are selling a product you must collect sales taxes from your customers. Whatever the sales tax is in your state, that amount must be added to the purchase price of the goods you are selling. In my home state of Georgia, sales tax is currently 3 percent, so an article retailing for $5.00 would cost the buyer $5.15 after the sales tax is added. If you dislike dealing with odd amounts you might wish to price your goods at $4.85 so as to bring your selling price to an even $5.00. That way you can simply label the product as costing $5.00 and you won't have to add anything else on. This makes the transaction somewhat smoother since you won't be needing to continuously make change. Regardless of which method you choose, you must keep accurate records.

In order to legally collect this tax, you must have a tax number assigned to your business. This number identifies you as a legally recognized collector of taxes. Contact your state capitol for the appropriate forms for obtaining your tax number.

Although all of us groan over paying taxes, this particular tax does provide one very helpful advantage. Once you have a tax number, you no longer have to pay sales taxes on goods you purchase for resale. You'll simply provide the tax number to the wholesaler, and he'll omit the sales tax on your purchase. For instance, suppose you buy pottery from a wholesaler, add your own decorative touches, insert a green plant, and sell the finished product. Once you have a tax number the sales tax is eliminated when you buy from the pottery wholesaler. Likewise the decorative paints, the baby plants, the potting soil, and even the calico bow are all products purchased for resale and are not subject to sales tax as long as you have your tax number.

Bookkeeping: The Business Side of Business

In spite of the aversion most people have to any sort of mathematical chores, a home business does require some bookkeeping. It's not sufficient merely to know what you're doing; you must have your business transactions substantiated on paper, too. This serves two purposes. First, you must be sure the Internal Revenue Service gets every penny that honestly belongs to it. Secondly, you must be sure the Internal Revenue does *not* get even a penny which honestly belongs to you. Keeping books might not be the most exciting part of a home business, but it is one of the most vital elements of your success. Taxes aren't especially thrilling to contemplate either, but if it's any consolation to you, throughout history millions of people have had the same problem. Taxes were also around during the earthly lifetime of Jesus and He set an example for us regarding payment (see Matt. 17:24–27).

HOW DO I START?

Although a professional system of bookkeeping is lovely to behold and is a delight to auditors, don't panic if you don't even know the meaning of double-entry bookkeeping.

Fortunately, successful money management does not hinge on the method, but rather it hinges on the result. You can use any method of bookkeeping which is convenient for you as long as your system is accurate, legible, and consistent.

If you want to be truly professional, you might find it a good investment to hire an accountant to set up your books for you and to show you how to keep your records. However, the "right" way is not the only workable way to keep books, so if you have an accurate system, don't feel you must change it.

Your personal record keeping can be either as simple or as complicated as you wish it to be. The important thing is just do it and do it right! Record every transaction and maintain a file of substantiating receipts. If ledger books intimidate you, you can use a notebook instead. Write down the date, the transaction, and the expense or income. Basically that is all there is to bookkeeping—just an accurate written record backed up by receipts, cancelled checks, and so on for proof.

WHAT MUST I RECORD?

1. Expenses. Expenses are the things you must buy in order to carry on your business. Let's look at my record keeping as an example. As a writer, some of my expenses are paper, typewriter ribbons, carbon paper, envelopes, and postage. These are things without which my product could not be produced. Therefore, I am legally entitled to deduct from my income any expense I incur on the way to making that income. Each time I buy one of those items, I obtain a receipt showing the name of the store where the item was purchased, the date of the purchase, and the amount of the purchase. Each of these expenses is noted in my ledger and each receipt is filed in an appropriately labeled envelope for easy retrieval at tax time.

2. Deductions. Deductions are similar to expenses, except that deductions are not actually part of the raw material used in the making of the product. Instead, deductions are business related expenses which the IRS allows you to subtract from your income. For example, each time I drive to an interview I record my mileage before leaving home and then record it again when returning. When a car is driven for business purposes, a mileage deduction of seventeen cents per mile is allowable for tax purposes. However, since mileage has no "paper" to back it up as proof for the IRS, you must be extremely careful to substantiate your mileage claim. Don't merely write down the number of miles; record the date as well as the purpose of the trip. You can buy inexpensive mileage notebooks which can be kept in your car just for this purpose.

Although the deductions you can claim will vary depending on the type of business you have, you can deduct such things as rent and utilities for your home office, as well as expenses for professional publications and professional dues, and even gifts and entertainment related to your business. Again, be prepared to substantiate these claims if called on to do so. If you have expenses which you feel should be subtracted from your taxable income, check with the Internal Revenue for the final authority on details related to your particular circumstances.

3. Profits. You *must* keep accurate records of every dollar your business takes in. To report less income than you actually made, makes you guilty of tax evasion, and there is a possibility of a jail sentence for that!

Although every dollar you take in is not truly profit, you must record every transaction where money comes into your hands. Your real and taxable profit will be the amount of money left at the end of the year after all expenses and deductions have been subtracted. That's why recording all those expenses and deductions is so vitally important.

That Dirty Nine-letter Word— Housework

A STUMBLING BLOCK TO SUCCESS?

Most women who begin a career at home find the first stumbling block to success is right under their noses—or at least right under their feet in the form of dust, dirt, and disorder. So, who cares? We do. In spite of those awful cartoons which usually depict housewives as abominable creatures adorned with hair curlers and bathrobes, most homemakers do genuinely care about their homes. Although it's not advisable to be like Martha and become so involved with household tasks that it becomes impossible to see beyond cooking and serving duties, maintaining a livable home is a priority with most women. The Bible even contains some advice on that subject. Proverbs 31:27 describes the virtuous woman's housekeeping: "She looketh well to the ways of her household, and eateth not the bread of idleness." Certainly a home business makes demands on a homemaker's time but even a successful business is not a sufficient excuse for failure to "look well to the ways of your household."

Some of the difficulty arises from the fact that a home business is done at *home,* while a public job takes you away from the house for a major portion of the day. When you are away from home all day, your thoughts are on business matters and it's relatively easy to dismiss thoughts of unmade beds and unwashed dishes. However, when you are involved in a home business the situation changes. No matter how you try to rationalize that your business is just as important as your housework, every time you turn around you feel a silent reproach flung at you by those unfinished chores. It's hard to ignore a sinkful of dishes if you have to pass through the kitchen twenty times a day.

Besides, staying at home full-time even creates more household chores. When I worked in a bank, I went out to lunch, so there were no lunch dishes to wash. Yet, being at home all day now adds the two chores of making lunch and washing extra dishes. Likewise, at the bank, if I spilled something on the floor, the janitor was summoned to clean up the mess. Life is just a bit different for the homeworker.

IS IT A WASTE OF TIME?

In recent years, the feminists have scoffed at the responsibility of keeping a clean house. Housekeeping is looked on as a degrading task, and homemakers are urged to ignore housework and spend time instead "fulfilling" themselves. With so many points of view being vehemently expressed, even a dedicated homemaker can become confused about how she feels on the subject of housework. Is it really a waste of time and talent to devote yourself to caring for a home and family? Admittedly, even a homemaker who actually loves housecleaning chores can occasionally become bored with the same old routine day after day. But boredom is no indication that the work is not worthwhile. Sometimes at 6:00 a.m. on rainy Monday mornings, I am less than thrilled at the prospect of housecleaning, but neither was I always thrilled at 6:00 a.m. on Monday mornings when I had to go to work at the bank. Boredom comes, not from the worth of the job, but from the sameness of an unvarying routine.

DOES HOUSEWORK WASTE MY TALENT?

The feminists also claim that mundane housework "stifles" talents and abilities. Yet, Romans 8:28 applies to the homemaking situation, too. Just because you now spend your days vacuuming and dusting, does not mean your talents and abilities won't be usable later on. (I sometimes think about the hours I spent studying Spanish, and I often wonder if I'll ever get a chance to use that skill. Nevertheless, where there's a will, there's a way, so I just say "Buenas dias, señorita Fluffy" and keep in practice. The cat doesn't seem to mind at all.) God allows us to learn Spanish, or typing, or piano playing for a purpose, and even if a talent isn't used today there's no reason to believe that the talent won't come in handy at a later date. Maybe that particular skill was included in the learning process as a tool for helping us find a way to stay at home *and* have a career at the same time. For this reason, it helps to look at housekeeping, not as a chore but as a tool for learning discipline and organizational skills. Every task in a person's life contributes to the shaping of his or her life. Perhaps David didn't readily understand the relationship between being a shepherd and being a king, but in God's plan for his life tending sheep was a vital step toward preparing David for the future. Likewise, even the oft-scorned task of keeping house can serve its purpose in God's plan for a homemaker's life.

The Christian homemaker who loves her home and wants to keep her family contented cannot abandon her duties at home in order to attempt a moneymaking project unless she is willing to sacrifice her own contentment at the same time. I've learned that whenever I sit down at my typewriter without first taking care of my household responsibilities, I don't accomplish much. No matter how hard I try to concentrate on writing, my mind wanders back to those jobs that need doing. In order to have a productive day, my only solution is to get up and take care of the chores first. Then when I do get down to business with the typewriter my conscience is clear.

You may have a somewhat different idea about housework. But no matter how much or how little housework you are accustomed to doing, once you start a home business, you *must* get organized or the home business will not work out.

HOW TO COPE

Let's find out just exactly what we are going to do about that dirty word, *housework*. Everybody gets twenty-four hours a day to work, eat, sleep, and relax. Since that's the limit we have to work with, the challenge comes in putting as much as possible into those twenty-four hours while maintaining a cheerful and lovable disposition.

First, decide what your housekeeping priorities are. You are the only person who can do this; what is right for someone else may not necessarily be right for you. Your own personal standards of what constitutes a clean house are the only guidelines you need follow. There's no magic formula for keeping house, however, in ten years of conducting home businesses while keeping a clean (or at times semi-clean!) house, I've found a method which works well for me.

I can't tolerate dirty dishes, unmade beds, clutter, dirty laundry, or obvious dirt. That means that in order to keep my personality lovable I must daily make my bed, wash the dishes, pick up clutter, do the laundry, and take out the garbage. These things are the absolute necessities of housekeeping as far as I'm concerned. Depending on your own personal approach to housecleaning, you probably think I'm either a compulsive housekeeper or a slob. That's the point! Everyone has to set her own standards.

After deciding what your housekeeping priorities are, the next step is to set up a schedule. Although my own schedule is far from perfect, it works reasonably well for me. Since I've already mentioned my idiosyncracies regarding daily chores, you're probably wondering how I handle the bigger nondaily tasks.

GETTING ORGANIZED

For me, Monday is not a good day for writing, but it's just right for cleaning house. Why? If your family is like mine and all of them were at home during the weekend, you may have noticed things usually aren't spic and span by Monday morning. This is especially true if your weekends, like ours, are filled with church activities and leisure pursuits. Since I don't do any unnecessary cleaning other than bed making, dish washing, and so on during weekends, Monday morning finds my house looking as if it needs my undivided attention. Therefore, I devote my Mondays exclusively to housecleaning and fill my hours with such tasks as vacuuming, polishing furniture, scrubbing walls, cleaning closets, and taking on any other house job that needs doing. Admittedly, Monday is my least favorite day of the week, but after all the chores are done I have the satisfaction of knowing the house is thoroughly clean, and I can do something besides clean house for the next few days.

Tuesday, Wednesday, and Thursday are the days I stay at my typewriter. I cook breakfast, pack lunches, wash a load of laundry, make my bed, and wash and dry dishes before I drive Karen to school. Then as soon as I get home I put the clothes in the dryer and plan what I'll cook for supper. With these two chores accomplished, I head straight for the typewriter and stay there the rest of the time Karen is in school. I stop work only long enough to take the clothes out of the dryer, to eat lunch, and to go to the mailbox. This gives me six hours a day for my work. I've found that eighteen hours a week is an adequate amount of work time for me.

OTHER CHORES

Friday is designated as my "goof off" day. Actually, there's no goofing off involved, but it makes me feel better to think of Fridays that way. Friday is the day I buy groceries, run errands, shop, go to the beauty shop (once every six months, that is!), or go to the dentist. As every homemaker knows, a wife who stays home automatically inherits the task of errand running, so rather than grieve and fret over it, I just set aside a day specifically for that purpose.

In addition to running errands on Fridays, I try to vacuum the house (just floors—the walls, drapes, and furniture get attention only on Mondays), dust, and in general get the house looking presentable for the weekend. Of course, with all those things to do, plus all the errands to run, I don't have time to cook, so Friday is the night we go out to eat. If your family is in the habit of going out to eat one night a week, you, too, might find it helpful to schedule your dining out time for a day when it will benefit your schedule the most.

TIME FOR CHURCH AND FAMILY

What about weekends? For us, Saturday and Sunday are reserved for family and church activities with an occasional civic or school function thrown in, too. Weekend activities are always those that our whole family can participate in. Sometimes our only Saturday activity is planting a garden or washing the car or going to the library, but whatever the event is, we choose something the three of us can share.

Sunday is for us a church day and a day for relaxing. My Sunday housework is minimal, just bed-making, cooking, and dishwashing. I believe the "recharge" I get from a day of rest will, in the long run, be of more benefit to me than any amount of work I might do on that day.

This is my way of taking care of my housekeeping responsibilities while conducting a home business. All of my ideas might not work for you, but they can serve as a starting point in your own planning. Do whatever fits you and your family best. Just be consistent and stay with a schedule that works. It's the only way you can successfully run a home business without having the home business run you.

You Have to Feed the Natives

When I first began my home business, the aspect of homemaking that gave me the most problem was cooking. The real problem wasn't the cooking—it was my attitude about cooking. I really love to cook, and for me a fun-filled day was one in which I produced several dozen homemade yeast rolls, a "scratch" cake, and a main dish that had been blended and stirred with tender loving care. Naturally, my family felt pampered by all these good things to eat. Consequently, when I became involved with home businesses, I had a problem. I could not take a family who was accustomed to that kind of cooking and turn them into fans of canned foods and frozen TV dinners.

WHAT'S THE PROBLEM?

You aren't successful as a home businesswoman if your family is constantly moaning, "We never have anything good to eat around here anymore."

Food is more than something to eat. It is symbolic of your family and of how each member of the family feels about his home. Think about some of the happiest times of your childhood. Aren't a good many of your pleasant memories tied up with food? Remember those special Thanksgiving dinners? How about those homemade cookies your mother had ready for you after school? What about those picnics by the lake—the ones that were so memorable that to this day you can't look at a bowl of potato salad without feeling a pleasant tingle of nostalgia?

Those are the reasons the food issue is so important when you have a home business. I don't understand all the psychological implications involved, but I can tell you this: your family won't see your new speedy meals as an abandonment of old-style cooking—they'll see those hurry-up meals as an abandonment of them. Of course, that attitude seems unfair to the aspiring homeworker, but that's the way families are, and if you can accept their attitude at the start of your home business, it will insure a minimum of trauma for everyone.

HOW CAN I COOK AND OPERATE A BUSINESS, TOO?

More than any other room in the house, the kitchen must be well-organized. If you're going to dash in, cook a good meal, and get finished in a minimum of time, the arrangement of the kitchen must work for you and not against you. For me, this means keeping my countertops as clear of clutter as possible in order to speed up the work. Too much time is wasted if I have to search for a place to put things down.

The second key to good organization is to get rid of kitchen items you don't use. In my family we seem to have an inherited weakness for saving plastic margarine tubs. (My aunt says we all own the same kind of family heirloom china—plastic margarine bowls!) For some reason those things seem to multiply overnight at my house. While one or two are handy to store leftovers in, twenty or thirty become clutter, not resourcefulness. Maybe you too, have your own way of accumulating clutter, but getting rid of the excess can be a big step toward having an organized kitchen. (I switched to stick margarine—some habits can only be kicked with drastic action!)

Third, put some of your early business profits into updating your kitchen appliances. If a slow-cooking crockery pot or a dishwasher or a microwave oven would simplify your business life, then it's good business to invest in timesaving kitchen equipment.

Last, if at all possible, locate your office or shop in the room next door to your kitchen. You'll save yourself thousands of steps as you go back and forth to stir that simmering stew. Remember, steps saved equal time and energy saved, and time and energy saved equal more dollars earned.

WHAT CAN I COOK FAST?

For me, the secret of good meals has not been what I can cook quickly but rather what I can cook slowly. The homemaker with a business to tend will find her best friend in the kitchen is the main dish which slowly simmers unwatched all day while other matters are dealt with. Baked ham, roasts, casseroles, stews, and hearty soups are life and business savers. Main dishes such as these provide substantial meals with an "I care" appearance, but they don't tie you to long hours over the stove.

My strategy is to start planning and cooking supper as soon as I return from taking Karen to school. You, too, can actually be much more productive in your home business when you get the meal planning out of the way so that your mind isn't constantly coming back to that problem while you're trying to work.

WHAT ABOUT TREATS?

It is possible to run a home business and still find time to make "scratch" desserts for your family. Eliminating frosting is one big time saver—and calorie cutter. I've found that items like pound cake, applesauce loaf, banana bread, and brownies are just as welcome as are frosted cakes, yet I save time by eliminating the icing. Another plus for unfrosted desserts is that they are easy to freeze. Consequently, you can make two batches at the same time and freeze some for another day's use.

Cookies, too, can be streamlined. Choose recipes for varieties such as peanut butter cookies or oatmeal cookies. Not only will you save yourself the time-consuming task of chopping nuts and using cookie cutters, but your family will have a more nu-tritious snack, too.

An even better way to cope with snacks is to make the creating of them part of the entertainment, too. If your ten-year-old is like mine, anything she helps me cook tastes better to her than does anything I cook alone. Consequently, a batch of peanut butter cookies isn't just a treat, making them provides a chance for some mother-daughter togetherness. Besides, when we go at it in that manner, the time spent making cookies is subtracted off television watching time rather than off my working time. Since I believe in limiting television time, some of our cooking is a welcome diversion and certainly more beneficial than is sitting in front of a television screen.

Bread baking is the one cooking activity that doesn't seem to adapt well to a home business. I can't do it during the day because it takes too much time, and I don't want to do it in the evening because we really don't need fresh yeast rolls at 11:00 p.m. Consequently, I've had to do considerable experimenting to find time to occasionally make yeast breads.

No matter what your home business is, or how much you love it, you will have days when you can't stand the thought of the home business. You don't want to give it up, but you simply aren't in the mood for doing it. When I first started working at home, I thought I had to stick to the job whether I was in the mood or not. Later I discovered that an occasional day off can have an energizing effect on the business. Now, when I have a day when I cannot write, I try not to waste time trying. Instead, I put that day to good use by doing something else. While my hands are busily coping with a batch of yeast bread, my mind is free to roam and the usual result is that I wind up, not only with something good to eat, but with a new idea for a manuscript.

Friends
and
Other Distractions

DO FRIENDS AND BUSINESS MIX?

Although it seems unbelievable, it is possible that your friendships will suffer greatly when you become a home-worker. But you don't feel it's your fault, and your friends certainly don't think it's their fault, so who gets the blame for the difficulties?

WHAT'S THE PROBLEM?

The problem with friends and a home business had its roots in your lifestyle long before starting a home business ever entered your mind. Let's take a look at the lifestyle of the average full-time homemaker.

If your children are preschoolers, you probably out of sheer desperation, spend quite a bit of time consulting with other mothers. When you're cast in a new and unfamiliar role, such as motherhood, it's comforting to fellowship with others who are in a similar position and can sympathize with your insecurities and worries.

Gradually, as your children get older, you and your friends have less to commiserate about and finally reach the stage where you can actually talk for a whole fifteen minutes before some small person yells, "Mommy!" Then as more time passes your children and hers are old enough to play together contentedly. Then it seems only logical to spend several hours each week visiting, "just so the kids will have somebody to play with," you say. Do you see the pattern that is developing?

Eventually, the children are old enough to go to school and suddenly mother is left to entertain herself for six hours a day. Since housekeeping is no longer the time-consuming chore it was in grandma's day, even a very meticulous housekeeper is going to find a certain amount of spare time on her hands during school hours. Doesn't it seem logical to invite someone over for a cup of coffee? Maybe it's a cold, snowy day and a telephone chat would help cheer you up. Do you see where all this is headed?

Eventually, the children grow up and marry and you are back where you began—just you and Prince Charming. Yet, things are different than they were in the early days of your marriage. Now you have a houseful of gadgets to make keeping house for two people a breeze. The hours hang heavily on your hands. Wouldn't it be nice to get together with some friends once or twice a week for lunch? Slowly you begin to get back into the swing of things you abandoned while raising your family.

Regardless of what stage of your life you are in right now, one thing remains constant and unchanging—you always need the friendship and fellowship of other women.

CAN OLD PATTERNS BE CHANGED?

People are adaptable in many ways, but when it comes to changing established habits, sometimes it is easier to change the location of Mount Everest than to change your friends' ideas about how things are supposed to be. Remember they need you, too. During all those times of confiding in each other, crying on each other's shoulders, and sharing fears and dreams, a bond was established between you. They depend on you, and when you suddenly decide to terminate all the to-getherness in favor of cold cash, they feel hurt and rejected.

Friends do not take kindly to the feeling of being unwanted at your home. Nor do they become delirious with joy when you terminate a brief telephone conversation in order to get back to your work. Yes, you really do want a home business, but you want to keep your friends, too. It begins to look as if you have to face the old problem that "you can't have your cake and eat it, too."

Yet, Christians in particular know the value of friends. So many Bible verses remind us of brotherly love. We're even told that "a friend loveth at all times," and "there is a friend that sticketh closer than a brother." The Bible gives numerous examples of beautiful friendships: Ruth and Naomi, David and Jonathan, Paul and Silas. Yet, in spite of the diversities of the circumstances of these friendships, each pair had one thing in common. They loved each other during discouraging, depressing events in their lives. Each one had important responsibilities to attend to, but the friendships survived because each one fulfilled his responsibilities while maintaining close ties with his friend. Can't we do the same?

FINDING A SOLUTION

Like many of the problems we face, this one has a solution. The first step is to admit a problem exists. Some homeworkers let their friends take up time during business hours and then blame themselves or their families when business profits don't roll in. It's not easy to admit that too much socializing is the root of the problem, but once you make that admission you can stop blaming yourself for being either inefficient or unorganized. If having too many friends underfoot during business hours *is* truly the problem, settle the matter first within your own mind before trying to reform your friends.

How much does a home business mean to you? Is it for pleasure or is it essential for necessities? Whatever the reason for your business, if you've prayed about starting your home career and you've settled in your own mind that a home business is approved by the Lord, by your husband, and by your own conscience, then you can also win your friends' approval. As long as you are wishy-washy in your convictions, no one will respect your intentions. However, when you finally reach the point where you know you are doing what is right for your life, then without guilt, you can confront your friends and enlist their cooperation. (Do you really suppose Ruth would have sat around drinking coffee and eating pound cake knowing that Naomi was depending on her?)

Try to realize how your friends must feel as they learn you are no longer available for coffee breaks, shopping trips, and all day visits. Try to imagine how you would feel if the situation were reversed and one of your friends suddenly announced her intention to return to work. Wouldn't it leave a gap in your life?

Sit down with each friend and thoroughly explain to her your reasons for starting a home business. Tactfully explain that you'll miss the fellowship, but remind her you value her friendship highly and you'll still set aside times for being with her.

Be realistic enough to realize some of your friends will at first be angered by your decision. Others will be hurt and resentful. Some may even deliberately retaliate by trying to sabotage your money-making efforts. You may be reading this in a state of shock, ready to argue, "Oh, no! *My* friends aren't like that at all!" Yes, they are! All you have to do to verify this is to hang out your home business shingle and watch reality come home to roost immediately.

"But, why," you ask, "would real, honest-to-goodness friends act like that?"

Mostly because they are real, honest-to-goodness human beings, too. They don't really wish you failure, nor are they consciously being malicious. Rather, they are people who love you and enjoy being with you, and in spite of their love and good intentions, they are just a tiny bit jealous of your new self-sufficient streak. Today's woman not only has all the responsibilities and duties that always went with housekeeping, child-rearing, and marriage, but in addition she is exhorted to "Grow! Reach out! Fulfill yourself!" Some women are torn between their wish to be full-time homemakers and the world's wish to make them feel second rate for choosing homemaking. Then to add to the feeling of failure, along comes someone (you) with a terrific idea for making money, fulfilling her creative urges, and staying at home full-time. Do you realize how this makes your friend feel? Suddenly she feels like a drudge, a failure, and a phased-out rag mop. Understand her. Give her your love and support and eventually everything will work out for both your business and your friendship.

IDEAS THAT WORK

When I first began a home business, I had to learn the hard way about friendships and business. Not knowing an effective way to cope with interruptions, I often entertained friends for several hours, all the time fervently hoping they would hurry and go home. Then by the time they actually did leave, my stomach was tied in knots and my head was pounding. By that time I couldn't work—I was too sick. At first, I blamed my friends for my failures, but finally came the realization that my own lack of honesty with them was my real problem.

The telephone was an even greater obstacle to my home business. As a young Christian, I felt it was my duty to help my friends with their problems. Hour after hour I stayed on the phone listening to them pour out their troubles. Ultimately, I realized my nerves were not able to take the kind of situation in which I seemed trapped. The little bit of income I made was not worth the price I paid with short temper, headaches, stomach aches, and general grouchiness.

Finally, I decided to be totally honest about my dilemma. I called each of my friends and tactfully explained the situation to her. Every single one of them was sympathetic, supportive, and understanding. Only one thing was wrong—each friend assumed I meant other people, but not her!

I tried another tactic. Upon answering the telephone I would say, "I'm so glad you called, but I only have a few minutes to talk. Let's talk fast so we can cover everything in ten minutes!"

Having friends drop by unannounced can also cut into working hours. Eventually I learned to ask them to come into my workshop in order that I might continue to work while we talked. Another solution I discovered was to avoid coming home immediately after taking my daughter to school. Most all day visits begin at that time. After leaving Karen at school, I ran errands, did my shopping or went to the library. In a half hour or so, I would return home. By that time all of the friends with "coffee-klatsch" personalities were firmly planted at someone else's table and I could go about my work without interruptions.

Does it sound as though I've become cynical, cold, and friendless? I hope not. I have more friends now than ever before, and I feel that those friends respect me for doing what I know is right for my family and myself.

THE CHRISTIAN'S RESPONSIBILITY

There are times when interruptions should not be discouraged. We do have an obligation to help those who earnestly need our assistance. Matthew 25:34–36 says:

> Then shall the King say unto them on his right hand, Come, ye blessed of my Father, inherit the kingdom prepared for you from the foundation of the world: For I was an hungred, and ye gave me meat: I was thirsty and ye gave me drink: I was a stranger, and ye took me in: Naked, and ye clothed me: I was sick, and ye visited me: I was in prison, and ye came unto me.

These words should dispel all doubt as to the kinds of interruptions we should gladly accept. Verse 40 makes our duty plain: "And the King shall answer and say unto them, Verily I say unto you, Inasmuch as ye have done it unto one of the least of these my brethren, ye have done it unto me."

No preoccupation with earning money should ever take precedence over Christian obligations. In addition, I believe that when a Christian unselfishly cares for others, God will make a way for necessary chores to be accomplished. Each day has only twenty-four hours in it, but with the Lord's help the hours can be stretched to contain all necessary activities.

Finding
Time

Everything looks promising. You've decided on a home business, taken care of legal matters, enlisted the aid of the family, received your friends' blessings, and even organized the children into a cleaning team. Yet, in spite of all the organization and planning, there's still no grand opening day for your business. Why? You just don't have enough time.

Unfortunately, time is the one commodity that present day society seems shortest on. No matter how well you plan, it seems there's not enough hours to do everything that needs doing. Isn't there a solution?

IS TWENTY-FOUR ALL I GET?

Yes, there's a solution, and it's elementary. Whether you are the President of the United States or a ditch digger, twenty-four hours a day is all you get to work with.

Yet, you *can* find more time. The secret is to go back over your schedule and find time you've overlooked.

First of all, if you're a conscientious wife and mother, a good cook, a proficient housekeeper, a faithful church member, and a responsible citizen, you already have a full day even without adding the time-consuming extra duties of a home business.

Since the life you lead is satisfying to you, you don't really want to give up any of those activities. How can you possibly fit in even one more responsibility?

SETTING TIME PRIORITIES

Again we come back to finding your priorities. Presumably by now you've determined what cooking, cleaning, family, and church activities must remain as they are in spite of a home business. By now, you're organized and motivated. Still, no big chunks of time are left over. Where *will* the time for the home business come from? You must "create" time where you assumed none existed.

ELIMINATING TIME WASTERS

In every life, there are always some activities which can be eliminated. However, if doing so is not right for you, you'll only cause yourself unhappiness. Therefore, the suggestions I'm offering are not iron-clad rules but are merely ideas to get you started thinking about your own circumstances.

My first timesaver was a new haircut. At one time my hair was shoulder length and had to be put up in electric curlers every morning. This took at least thirty minutes. Since long hair takes quite a while to dry after a shampoo I was spending four additional hours a week at that chore. Combing and styling took up an additional thirty minutes per day. When I began my home business I got a new ultra-short hairdo which can be blown dry in about ten minutes and requires absolutely no setting. A simple haircut changed my hair grooming time from eleven hours per week to less than one hour per week. I had gained ten hours of "extra" time for my home business each week!

My second timesaver was a limit on telephone conversations. Before beginning my home business, I had frequently spent as much (or more!) as two hours a day on the telephone. After I learned to talk ten minutes and get everything said, I discovered at least *twelve* extra hours per week available for me.

Third, I learned to leave the television alone. I guess daytime television watching is something that simply comes naturally to homemakers, especially if children are around. We count on it to entertain the little ones, and then we find ourselves getting absorbed in it, too. I used to enjoy folding laundry or ironing while watching "Captain Kangaroo," but I have to admit the jobs took much longer that way. Then, too, I felt I had to watch the news every day in order to be well informed. However, I later discovered that catching the radio news twice a day while driving Karen back and forth to school keeps me just as well informed without costing me any loss of working time. The result of my television limitation was a gain of ten to twelve hours added to each week.

These three simple timesavers added thirty-five hours to my week—and that's ample time for any home business. The best part of it, however, was that I didn't have to give up any of the things which were really important to me. I eliminated only time wasters.

LEARNING TO SAY NO

Yet, as time-adding as these three decisions were, the real bonus came when I learned to say no.

Mothers who do not work outside the home naturally become delegates for all sorts of school, church, and civic jobs that other people don't have time to do.

It's not easy to say no, especially if the cause is a worthwhile one. However, even a great man such as Charles Spurgeon realized that easy compliance with every request is a great time waster. In his book *John Ploughman's Talks,* Spurgeon says, "Learn to say 'no' and it will do you more good than being able to speak Latin."

This doesn't mean you should never say yes; it means you should have sense enough and backbone enough to know when the request is one that does not deserve a yes. For instance, if one of your children is in a club and the sponsor thinks it would be nice to have refreshments each week, should you be the only one to carry cupcakes to the meeting simply because you are a homeworker and the rest of the mothers work outside the home?

The same problem arises in church activities, too. In our church the deacon's wives are responsible for organizing the carrying of food to members' homes when there has been a death in the family. Since the other wives worked outside the home and I did not, I went along for years never questioning the wisdom of having to do all the calling by myself. Then one weary day after I spent all day making calls to more than forty people, I realized how ridiculous the situation was. My husband had a talk with the other deacons, and it was agreed to divide the responsibility so that no one had to make more than a few calls. I learned a lesson from that. Sometimes nobody helps because nobody knows you want to be helped. Learn to say no, and, at the same time, spread the responsibility around. Don't be shy about asking for help when you need it. Give somebody else a chance to share a blessing!

YOUR SELF-IMAGE

Probably the main reason home businesswomen have so much trouble finding time is because of the lack of a confident self-image. It's easy to feel professional when you go out to work each day. After all, doesn't your tweed suit and silk blouse show you mean business about business? It's not that easy to feel like you mean business when you're at home all day in a pair of faded jeans and grass-stained tennis shoes.

Nevertheless, it's not the clothes, but the attitude, that makes the business successful. You can't successfully run a home business until you realize that in spite of having no time clock, no dress code, and no commuting, you *are* truly in business. You have to have a positive outlook yourself or you cannot expect anyone else to respect what you're doing.

If you don't have the self-discipline to see your business as a business rather than merely as an amusing hobby, no one else is going to take your business seriously either. If you dropped in on a friend who didn't seem to care one way or the other if she finished the task she was involved in, would you feel too guilty about disturbing her? If, however, your friend was friendly and cordial, but invited you into her workshop and kept right on working, wouldn't you get the message that she was in business and serious about it? No one is going to esteem your work any higher than you do. If you don't have a confident self-image, why should anyone treat you as a professional?

TIME AS A REWARD

Yet, in spite of being business-like and professional, and in spite of being able to say no, there are certainly numerous times when someone needs you, and to refuse them would be entirely selfish.

How can you tell when the need is genuine? It takes practice, but if you'll take time to analyze the situation, you'll soon develop an ability to distinguish between what is a real need and what is not. Let's suppose you have a friend named Martha, who was a successful career woman until the birth of her baby two years ago. Now she is a full-time homemaker, not because she wants to be, but because her husband insists. Martha feels cheated by having to stay home all day alone with a two-year-old. Consequently, she insists she deserves a day off once a week to go shopping. Would you mind if she brought her baby over for you to keep from eight o'clock this morning until five this afternoon? Of course, we all know two-year-olds, and Martha's is no different from anyone else's. He's almost potty trained, but not quite. He puts everything in his mouth. He yells, "No!" every chance he gets. He pulls the dog's ears and walks on the cat's tail. He's too old for a nap and too young to do without one. What are you going to tell Martha?

Now do you really think the Lord ought to bless you with the gift of extra time when you have no more backbone than to get yourself into a mess like that?

However, if the need is genuine, saying no to Martha would be wrong. Suppose Martha's mother has the flu and is so sick that Martha must go over to sit with her. She calls and asks if you will babysit Junior. Of course, he's still the same rambunctious two year old, but the situation is radically different. Saying no in a case like that wouldn't help either your business or your Christian testimony.

The amazing thing about those occasions when help is genuinely required is that you'll probably get just as much work done even after you help your friend! How does that happen? I believe the Lord blesses your efforts at service and helps you get maximum productivity after the service is performed.

Don't you suppose that when the good Samaritan interrupted his trip long enough to care for some disabled stranger the Lord blessed his efforts? Most likely as he went on his journey his donkey got more miles per bale of hay than ever before, and, in spite of the detour, the Samaritan reached his appointment on time.

Don't ask for an explanation of how you can take two hours out of a six-hour work period in order to help a friend and then still manage to accomplish six hour's worth of work. Don't try to understand it—just accept it and rejoice in it!

How
Not to Go
Into Business

When homemakers think of becoming at-home career women they seem to inevitably think of their future prospects in a rosy, glowing manner. A home business can be enjoyable and profitable or it can be a total flop. Therefore, it's not realistic to talk about home businesses without also mentioning ideas which simply do not work.

WHAT ABOUT THOSE ADS?

You don't have to read the advertising columns many times to discover the ads aimed directly at homemakers, retirees, and the handicapped. Most of the ads read something like this:

EARN BIG MONEY AT HOME!!!
Make money at home. No
experience necessary.
Details $2.00.
Box 234, Anywhere, U.S.A.

What is wrong with this ad? First of all, notice that there is nothing illegal about it. The ad doesn't actually promise you a job, so even after you waste your two dollars you have no legal grounds for complaint. Of course, these ads are worded so as to cause you to reach conclusions profitable for the advertiser, but as long as he doesn't actually promise something and then fail to deliver it, the ads are within the bounds of the law.

What will you get if you do decide to "invest" your money? Most likely a pamphlet, telling you a half dozen ways to make money—all of which you already knew but had ruled out as impractical ways to go into business. You might also receive a list of companies that supposedly will hire you to type or stuff envelopes or make phone calls. The catch is that this "employment" comes only after you buy a list of prospects, most of which will be duds.

A variation on the offer to sell information is the ad which comes right out and tells you what kind of job is being offered. The most common one is envelope stuffing. Theoretically, anyone can stuff envelopes, so this type of work will appeal to both handicapped people and people with limited education. These ads lead you into the same useless circles. You are promised, for a fee, a list of companies which supposedly need your services. The only problem is that none of the companies do need your services. Either the companies have gone out of business, or they hired an envelope stuffer one time and that was ten years ago.

Although some of the ads are frauds, most of them stay barely within the limits of legality. Consequently, there's little you can do if you've been taken in. The promoters of those schemes count on most people who respond being too embarrassed to admit that they have been taken. And for the small sum of money which has been lost, most people aren't willing to prosecute even if the ad was fraudulent.

Of course, it would cost you more to prosecute than you would likely recover, but if you've been deceived by a clearly fraudulent ad, report the matter to the Better Business Bureau and to the Post Office Department. Mail fraud is a federal crime, and the penalties are rather stout. You won't have to bear the expense of prosecution either. Postal inspectors will handle the investigation and the court case.

WHAT ABOUT MAIL ORDER?

Probably no business in the world carries a higher failure and heartbreak rate than does the mail-order business. The business itself is actually a good one, but too many inexperienced people with too high expectations are taken in by too many unscrupulous suppliers whose schemes do not work. Again, you'll be likely to see plenty of ads offering to teach you how to amass a fortune in mail order. Fortunes *have* been made in mail order, but not usually by the beginner who has to buy his product from someone else who may or may not be honest.

Mail order can be a highly successful home business provided it is approached in a logical and cautious manner untinged by the greed to get rich quick. The important things to remember are: begin with a quality product; start on a small, realistic scale; buy only from reputable list brokers; and *never, never* invest more cash than you can safely afford to lose.

WHAT ABOUT CREATING A PRODUCT FOR RESALE?

Another favorite ploy of the unscrupulous promoters of work-at-home schemes is to persuade people to create a product, which will presumably be bought back at great profit to the worker. The plan goes like this: First, you buy the raw materials to make the product. Naturally, they are over-priced, but you are told these goods must be used exclusively to make the product, because any other materials will not meet the buyer's specifications. Then you create the product, and return it to the supplier. The supplier refuses to accept what you have made. He says you have not done the type of quality workmanship he can accept.

Where does this scheme leave you? Not only are you out the money you spent on materials, but you've wasted your time and in the process acquired a product you can't possibly sell elsewhere. The result? You don't make money—you lose it.

Any honest, legitimate company which allows workers to do work at home does not charge for the materials used. Regardless of what kind of piecework you are doing at home, you should be supplied the materials free of charge and then paid for labor only. Although it is possible to find these kinds of reputable jobs, there is a scarcity of them.

WHAT ABOUT TELEPHONE SOLICITATION?

Telephone solicitation is another one of those jobs that practically everyone thinks she can do. Certainly, some reputable companies do utilize this method of contacting customers, but even under the best of circumstances, telephone soliciting can be a nerve-wracking job. Remember, not everyone will be polite. You'll hear language you never knew existed, and you'll receive propositions for every kind of activity the human mind can devise.

However, the people you contact can't cause you as much grief as can the people for whom you work. In the first place, many of the companies who use telephone solicitors don't pay unless you make a sale. Unless you're really adept at selling, you may work for days and days without making any money at all. Not only that, many companies require you to high pressure those with whom you talk, and that certainly isn't Christlike behavior.

The really detrimental result lies in how the job may effect your Christian testimony. Could you live with your conscience if you knew you had talked someone with little income into buying an inferior product he could ill afford? How would you feel if the product you were promoting turned out to be defective or even dangerous?

If you *must* do telephone solicitation, work only for established companies. Check on them with the Better Business Bureau and the Chamber of Commerce. Never get involved with soliciting for land purchases, investment speculations, or questionable home improvement products. Depending on the circumstances, *you* could be arrested, too, as an accomplice. A few dollars aren't worth that risk!

WHAT ABOUT RECRUITING OTHERS?

A variation on the telephone soliciting theme is the recruitment of people to invest in something you have already bought. The scheme works like this: You buy ten shares in a company. Then you are told that if you recruit ten more people to take part in the "great opportunity" you will get your money back. It sounds good, doesn't it? In exchange for a little selling to your friends, you'll get back the money you spent plus a big profit, and, at the same time, you'll still own the shares. There's one thing seriously wrong with this plan. Each person who invests gets the same opportunity you were given. Each new investor is asked to recruit ten more investors. Can you see where this is leading? Very shortly the participants have grown in number to an astronomical figure and the whole scheme collapses. If you're one of the early participants you might not lose money, but as the pyramid grows later participants are required to support those already in the program, and, if you come in further down the line, you're certain to lose.

These schemes are called pyramids and are illegal. However, the promoters also know that what they are doing is illegal, so as soon as things begin looking bad, the promoters pack up all the money and leave town. In many cases the promoters are so accomplished in this type of fraud that it's impossible to catch up with them and have them arrested.

Investment schemes are popular but other ideas for pyramid selling are used, too. Sometimes you're asked to buy "distributorships." You sell a product and collect a percentage of the selling price as your profit. Then if you recruit others to sell the product you get a percentage of their profits, too. In theory, eventually you reach the point where you are doing no work at all, but are receiving a tremendous income from all the people who are working for you. The only problem is that each of your "employees" has the opportunity to also become distributors instead of salesmen if only they are willing to recruit others.

The result of any pyramid scheme is that you lose. Even if you manage to get back your money, you still lose. What do you suppose your recruitment is going to do to your Christian testimony? How will your friends feel about losing their money because they listened to your persuasive talk?

Questions About Home Businesses

No matter how thorough a writer tries to be, inevitably many questions are left unanswered. Certainly, I can't cover every question you might have about home businesses, but I would like to share with you some answers to questions frequently asked by women who want to get started in a home business.

WHERE CAN I GET THE MONEY?

My advice to would-be entrepreneurs is to never invest more money in any business than what you can safely afford to lose. Admittedly, when you're all excited about a new endeavor, it's hard to come down to earth and admit the whole idea might not work. Nevertheless, hold onto all your enthusiasm, and season it with common sense. Too many good ideas have been ruined by someone trying to start a business on a scale too grand for practical purposes. A shoestring beginning means you have a real struggle ahead, but when you have meager beginnings you quickly develop a real knack for learning to make do. Accordingly, I suggest you start small and expand cautiously as your finances permit.

However, if you feel you simply must have more financing than you can muster on your own, there are ways to get the cash you need. The Small Business Administration can be of valuable help to you in obtaining funds. The SBA makes low interest loans to help fledgling businesses, but various stipulations must be met. The SBA will not loan money for all kinds of businesses—publishing is a business which the SBA will not help financially. Another stipualtion is that you must not use the borrowed funds to pay off other debts. So if you're going to borrow from the SBA, don't plan on using the money to pay off higher interest loans you've acquired elsewhere. Since requirements for SBA loans change from time to time the best source of action would be to write to the Small Business Administration and ask about current requirements. You will need to prepare a financial statement showing your assets, liabilities, and net worth in order to apply for a loan from the SBA.

WHERE CAN I GET BUSINESS ADVICE?

One of the most valuable sources of help is the Service Corps of Retired Executives, more commonly known as SCORE. SCORE is a service of the Small Business Administration and is made up of retired businesspeople who, free of charge, offer counseling to people who have small businesses. If you live anywhere near a city of reasonable size, chances are there is a chapter of SCORE within your reach. Contact the nearest office of the SBA for more information.

IF I DON'T NEED MONEY, DO I STILL NEED THE SBA?

Even if you never borrow a cent nor ever have need for the services of SCORE, the Small Business Administration can be of valuable assistance to you. The SBA publishes numerous books and pamphlets which are invaluable to a beginning businessperson. The pamphlets are free and there is only a small charge for the books. The SBA publications cover every aspect of home businesses and small businesses in general. The free publications range in subject matter from selling products on consignment to managing a family-owned business.

SHOULD I FORM A CORPORATION?

Most of us have grown accustomed to thinking of corporations as giant companies with branch offices across the country, huge advertising budgets, and thousands of employees. Yet a corporation can also be very small, local, without an advertising budget, and run by only one person. A corporation is formed usually for two purposes: 1. *To protect your personal assets.* If your business is a corporation and someone decides to sue you, you may lose all your business, but you can't lose your personal property such as your home or your personal savings account. Additionally, debts or bankruptcy of the corporation has no bearing on your own personal credit rating. 2. *To gain tax advantages.* If you have a sole proprietorship (you personally own and control the business) you must pay taxes on all the profits of the business yourself. If, however, your business is incorporated, you pay taxes only on the salary paid to you as an employee of the corporation. The corporation pays a separate tax for itself.

Although incorporation may be a wise step for the home businesswoman who is successfully established in a highly profitable endeavor, it may not be worth the trouble for the small-scale home business. Corporations are taxed at a much higher rate than are sole proprietorships. Also, there are considerably more regulations to abide by and more government forms to cope with. For the best advice in your particular case, consult the SBA, SCORE, or a competent attorney or accountant.

HOW DO I GET A COPYRIGHT?

To most people the idea of a copyright brings to mind visions of mountains of paperwork, teams of lawyers, and plenty of expenses. Getting a copyright is not a complicated procedure at all. Many people handle the procedure themselves.

Copyrights are most generally thought of in connection with written material, such as manuscripts. However, copyrights may be obtained on varying types of material. You can copyright music or even patterns or designs.

The laws regarding copyright have been revised in recent years and on January 1, 1978, new copyright laws went into effect. The new laws give the holders of copyrights more legal protection now than ever before. Anything copyrighted after January 1, 1978, extends the copyright to the owner's lifetime plus an additional fifty years.

The cost of obtaining a copyright is ten dollars. This fee must be sent to the Copyright Office, Library of Congress, Washington, DC 20559, along with the appropriate form for the type work you wish to copyright. Before sending any money, write first and ask which form you will need. If you feel you need more help, ask for the current circulars dealing with the copyright law and for a copy of the law itself.

HOW DO I GET A PATENT?

Obtaining a patent is somewhat more involved than getting a copyright. There are several classifications under which a patent may be granted, and sometimes it's difficult to determine exactly which category your invention falls into. Also, getting a patent involves a certain amount of investigation to determine that your gadget is truly an original one. Drawings and diagrams must be submitted along with the description.

For most people, consulting an attorney (a patent attorney if possible) is the best course of action, because the average person is not sufficiently experienced in law to capably deal with a patent application. If, however, you feel you'd like to try doing this on your own, one of the best books on the subject is *Techniques for Preparing and Obtaining Your Own Patent* by Hrand M. Muncheryan.

SHOULD I SELL ON CREDIT?

Although cash is the best basis for any small business, if you become quite successful you may find yourself in a situation that calls for the consideration of credit. If you produce a product in quantity, wholesalers may want to buy bulk shipments and then have you bill them in thirty days. Consequently, if your sales are credit sales, some of your purchases of raw materials may have to be on credit, too.

Credit is useful if handled properly, but it is an area that can cause a great deal of grief if misused. Therefore, if you're planning to get involved in credit buying and selling, do so on a limited scale and exercise all possible caution.

Don't extend credit to anyone whom you have not checked thoroughly. The Better Business Bureau can tell you if a firm has had complaints lodged against it for bad debts. Also, Dun and Bradstreet lists thousands of corporations and their credit ratings. If a firm has a less than spotless record, a small business, such as yours, can easily be hurt by either nonpayment or excessively slow payment.

Perhaps you've also wondered about extending credit to individuals. The safest policy is—don't. When I had a dressmaking business, credit was a question that came up frequently. I tried to be as polite as possible, but on the subject of payment, I had one inflexible rule. No garment could leave my home until that garment had been paid for in full. Most people don't mind this policy as long as you let them know that it is your way of doing business with everyone and not just some rule you've made up for them alone. I always made it a point to discuss this matter with new customers in advance of doing any work for them because I felt it was better to answer the question *before* it was asked. (Once a customer didn't have the money to pay for two blouses I had made for her. I told her I could not let them leave my house without payment. She replied that she understood my policy and would get them when she had the cash to pay for them. One year later she arrived to pay for her blouses!)

If you cannot avoid extending credit, the only safe way to do so is by offering customers charge card privileges. Of course, this service costs you money, which in the long run must be passed on to your customers through increased prices. However, our society has become so plastic card oriented that customers practically demand charge privileges. If you do decide to go the credit card route, choose a company which issues cards that are usable nationwide. You'll have to pay a fee to get started, plus a monthly fee, plus a percentage of each transaction (usually three percent).

HOW CAN I GET A CREDIT RATING?

If you've ever purchased anything with time payments, you've already established a credit record. This means that your local or regional credit bureau has a file on your credit history. However, most women don't have a credit rating because houses, cars, and charge accounts are usually in husbands' names.

If you want to establish a credit rating for yourself, go to the bank and borrow a sum of money—perhaps two to five hundred dollars. Of course, the bank isn't going to be thrilled over having you as a customer, since, as far as credit goes, you are an unknown. However, most banks will let you have the loan readily enough if you handle the transaction in a manner that is risk-free for them. To do this, you borrow the money, open a savings account with it, and put the savings account up for collateral of the loan. The bank has nothing to lose in a case like this, because they know that even if you fall down on the payments they can confiscate the account and get their money back. Admittedly, it seems strange to borrow money to open a savings account, but if you're new to the world of credit, this method may be the only way you can get started on establishing a credit rating for yourself. Remember, too, that you'll actually lose a little money in the process because the interest rate on the loan might be more than 10 percent while the interest rate on the savings account may be as low as 5 percent.

If you need to establish credit on the commercial level, you'll need to be listed in Dun and Bradstreet. Write to this organization and request appropriate forms to be filled out for consideration in their publication.

HOW CAN I HANDLE BAD CHECKS?

A large corporation with a multi-million dollar inventory can readily absorb a number of losses from bad checks, but the homeworker who is struggling to make a few extra dollars can ill afford to see a whole day's labor lost by even one bad check.

Checks are a fact of life in our modern society so it's impossible to run a business without accepting them, especially if you are going to deal with a large number of clients.

As in other aspects of home businesses, the best policy is

professionalism. If you must take checks, require identification from those you do not know. (Obviously, if you're doing something such as teaching piano playing and you'll see the same customer week after week, requiring identification will only make you look silly. I am talking about requiring identification in situations such as at a craft show where all the customers are unknown to you.) Certainly, requesting a driver's license number and credit card number will not guarantee that the check will be good, but it does serve the psychological purpose of making the customer think you'll track him down if the check is bad.

In most cases, the amount of a check may be too small to warrant the time and trouble to pursue the matter further. However, you can keep sending a bounced check back through the customer's account until the piled up insufficient funds charges convince him that you are not giving up. Then if he closes the account or stops payment on the check, you'll have grounds for prosecuting him.

When I ran my dressmaking business, I told all my customers that checks were inconvenient for me and that I must be paid in cash. Since at that time I did not drive I explained that getting to the bank to cash checks was difficult for me. However, on some occasions I did accept checks from customers I knew and trusted. Once a new customer came to pick up the first garment I had made for her. As she handed me her check she asked, "Aren't you afraid to take checks from people you don't know?"

"Well, I guess it could be a risk," I told her, "but I'm not at all worried about taking a check from you."

"Oh!" she said smiling, "That's so sweet of you!"

"I'm afraid 'sweet' doesn't have much to do with it," I told her. "Remember, you brought me two sacks full of material which you want made into dresses. I noticed the cash register tape was for fifty dollars. If your check bounces, I will keep for myself two sacks full of lovely material."

I wonder why she always paid cash after that.

What Is
the $ Value
of Full-time Homemaking?

IS A HOME BUSINESS WORTH THE TROUBLE?

Perhaps as you've read through the how-to of starting a home business, you've become somewhat discouraged. "Wouldn't it be simpler to just take a job outside my home?" you ask.

Truthfully, in some ways a job outside the home *is* simpler. Running a successful home business requires initiative, persistence, and good planning. It's relatively simple to go to someone else's place of business, punch a time clock, return home, and resume family life. A career at home, in spite of its advantages, offers additional problems. The woman who works at home is constantly aware of her surroundings. Never mind that she's president of the XYZ Company—she's first and foremost a homemaker. While the wife and mother who works outside the home is no less diligent about her home responsibilities, she does have the advantage of being physically separated from worrisome home tasks for a major portion of the day. True, the coffee table still needs dusting when she gets ome after a day's work, but she hasn't had the psychological burden of having to look at it all day while at the same time trying to concentrate on her moneymaking task.

Sometimes, too, it is easier to have someone else as your boss. Being an employee relieves you of a majority of the business related headaches to which you fall heir when the business is your own. Decision making is a tiring task and some people simply are not emotionally able to tolerate the strain.

WHAT ARE THE ADVANTAGES?

If a career at home presents problems, why then would any woman want to make life difficult for herself? The answer varies with the individual, but the most common reasons for starting a home business rather than taking an outside job, are these: 1) a desire to put home and family first; 2) a need for a flexible schedule; 3) the belief that a mother working outside the home really doesn't make any money. Let's examine reason three more closely.

Most women find it incredibly hard to believe they could spend forty hours each week, diligently sacrificing their time and energy and yet have much, much, less than minimum wage to show for their efforts. Yet, in many cases, that's exactly the way things turn out.

Does it pay to work outside the home? Is it really more profitable to run a home business? Let's look at the money side of homemaking to see what the financial advantages are.

GOING BACK TO WORK

Some time ago I did a magazine article about the dilemma of trying to weigh the dollar advantage of an outside job against the dollar advantage of being a homemaker. The results were astonishing.

I discovered that the average homemaker entering the job market after a few years' absence could plan on receiving less salary than would a new high school graduate with no work experience. To test this point, I spent several weeks filling out applications and going to interviews in order to find out what the prospects were for women like me who had been out of the job market for a few years—in my case eight years.

Prospective employers seem to look with suspicion on any homemaker who has been away from a career for more than a year. Their reasoning? If you liked being unemployed for that long, chances are you'll soon tire of working, and they'll be left to find a replacement. That's costly for business, so interviewers try to find employees whom they hope will have "stickability."

Second, homemakers re-entering the business world often bring rusty skills and out-of-date attitudes. In my own case, I had previously held a supervisory job and not only knew how to operate different types of office machines, but I had also had the responsibility of training other employees. Yet, in spite of my experience, the new machines developed in the eight years I had been out of work were so different from what I had known that I could no longer even profess a working knowledge of them. Consequently, an inexperienced recent graduate of a business school would have had a better chance at getting any job for which I had applied.

The third thing which worries prospective employers is children. Every interviewer I met asked what my baby-sitting arrangements were. Other homemakers being interviewed have related stories of having an interviewer ask them if they planned to have any more children!

These three things—years of unemployment, rusty skills, and baby-sitting problems—make it difficult for women to get jobs outside their homes. Consequently, when an employer does decide to "take a chance" on you, he limits his potential loss by having you begin with a very small salary. In spite of eight years of inflation, I was offered jobs barely equal in pay to what I had made in my previous job. Grocery costs have doubled in those eight years, but salaries have not. These low starting salaries make it highly unprofitable for a woman to start a new career while her children are still at home, requiring a paid baby sitter.

WHAT ABOUT DEDUCTIONS?

Yet, in spite of meager beginning pay, even that modest sum is not what you have when you finally get home with the remains of your paycheck. There'll be social security deductions, federal tax, state tax, and maybe even some "optionals" you have to take. When union dues, mandatory charity contributions, and group insurance premiums also come out of the salary the results may be pitiful.

WHAT DOES IT COST ME TO WORK?

Added to the deductions are the expenses of merely getting back and forth to work, feeding yourself while you are there, and paying competent nursery help. Baby-sitting fees take a huge bite from a working mother's paycheck. Then, of course, there's a certain amount of increase necessary in your clothing allowance, because after all, you can't wear your paint stained slacks to the office.

If you work in a large city, you have to choose between time and money. Driving to work is faster than taking the bus, but then you have to add the expense of gasoline and parking. Lunches can be dealt with on the brown bag plan, but do you really have the initiative to add an extra chore to the morning's already hectic schedule? Can you be content with a peanut butter sandwich while everyone around you goes out for a steak? And expensive convenience foods begin appearing with regularity on your dinner table because there's no time to cook from scratch. These are just a few of the added expenses you'll encounter.

HOW MANY HOURS DOES IT TAKE TO MAKE FORTY?

It always surprises me to see how naive many women can be about the hours in a work week. "But I'll be away from home only for forty hours a week," they explain. Maybe that's true if your neighbor has a home business and you need only to go next door to work. Otherwise, you will have to plan on extra time away from home. Most businesses work eight hours a day, but you'll likely get an hour for lunch, so you wind up being at the job for nine hours, not eight. And transportation takes up more of your time. It's a fortunate person who lives near enough her work to get there in half an hour. Even if you can do this, you'll find that you're investing ten hours of your day in that eight-hour job. Divide ten hours into your bring-home pay to determine a more realistic figure as your true hourly wage.

Even after you leave your job and start toward home, it's doubtful that you'll be able to go straight there. Inevitably, you'll need to stop for gasoline or a loaf of bread or maybe your suit must be picked up at the cleaners. These things take extra time, so your eight-hour job separates you from your family, not eight hours a day, but ten or eleven!

WHAT IS THE DOLLAR VALUE OF THE FULL-TIME HOMEMAKER?

In contrast to the woman who works outside the home, the woman who is a full-time homemaker does not have the expenses of the working woman who is employed outside her home. Instead, the stay at home wife and mother may actually have "income" she does not even recognize. Have you ever tallied up the "salary" you receive as a full-time homemaker?

Let's look at some of the ways you can have an income.

Do you sew? If you do, have you ever stopped to calculate the dollar value of those home-sewn items? If you're an enthusiastic seamstress the value of your work may be worth thousands of dollars annually. Even a homemaker who sews only occasionally can value her work at several hundred dollars per year.

If you're like me, perhaps at one time or another, due to having more time than money, you tackled virtually every imaginable sewing task in the household. I've made suits for Randal; lingerie, coats, and dresses for Karen and me; and I've also grappled with draperies, quilts, and upholstery. Yet, even while I was proudly complimenting myself on saving money, I never thought to tally up the yearly total. Then one day, I did calculate the profit and the results were astonishing. Try it yourself. Calculate what it would cost you to go to work if you had to give up all that dollar-saving sewing. Of course, if you have a job outside your home you'll make time to do some sewing, but most likely your efforts won't be nearly as extensive as they are now.

Do you have a garden? Our county extension agent told me that even a modest investment in seeds—perhaps only ten dollars' worth—has the capacity of yielding up to three hundred dollars in groceries. Remember that your garden is "income," too, and it's tax free. If you had an outside job could you get home around six o'clock in the evening, put a good meal on the table, and then have the time and energy left for gardening?

Do you like to cook? The creative cook with a full day at home has the time to plan low-cost menus. A simmered all day pot of beans has plenty of protein, and the cost is certainly less than the cost of a hastily prepared expensive cut of meat.

Are you a good shopper? The full-time homemaker has the time and opportunity to take advantage of sales. While shopping at three grocery stores may provide real savings for you, the woman who works outside the home has no time for this type of comparison shopping. Also, by the time she gets to the grocery store the best cuts of meat are gone, the specials are sold out, and the lines are long. And she has lost an additional three or four dollars in savings if she didn't use her lunch hour to clip out those "cents off" coupons in the newspaper.

How do you cope with Christmas? Although most of us wail over the fact of Christmas becoming too commercialized, we still seem to get caught up in the lure of advertising. The full-time homemaker has an alternative. She has the time to sew a new dress for grandmother and a rag doll for a sister's child. She can give the pastor a jar of homemade jelly or pickles, and she can present Junior's teacher with a box of homemade fudge. She can macramé, decoupage, crochet, knit, or build her gifts instead of spending money at the store. Depending on how "crafty" she is, she can save quite a bit of money at the holiday season. (I calculate my homemade wedding, graduation, birthday, new baby, and Christmas gifts as an "income" of three to five hundred dollars per year.)

You see, homemaking has money-making potential, too. Don't forget to consider the income you already have before you abandon it and go out and take a job. Of course, taking a job at home instead of out of the home does not positively guarantee that you'll still have time for all these pursuits, but when you work at home your hours are flexible and you're much more likely to do these things than you would if you spent ten or eleven hours a day away from home.

TAKING A LOOK AT FINANCES

Just to help you determine how important your homemaking is, let's make a chart to see how being a full-time homemaker compares with being a working woman who spends fifty hours or more away from home each week. Of course, the results you achieve will depend entirely on your own lifestyle, but even if your "income" at home is not phenomenal, I believe the results will still be quite a surprise to you.

Fill in the blanks to suit your own circumstances and then you'll more clearly understand the advantages of a home business.

A Job Outside My Home

Gross wage
  minus
    social security
    federal tax
    income tax
    union dues
    charity donation
    insurance
  equals take-home pay
Take-home pay
  minus
    baby-sitting fees
    cost of gasoline
    cost of parking
    cost of bus riding
    lunches
    new clothes
    special cleaning of clothes
    convenience foods
  equals true net pay

The Dollar Value of Homemaking

Money earned from:
    sewing
    giftmaking
    comparison shopping
    repairs (such as reupholstery)
    gardening
    budget cooking
    coupon shopping
  equals income

Now subtract the homemaking income, which you'd give up with an outside job, from the net take-home income of a job outside your home. Perhaps you did better than I did. I came out with a total of $183 *per year* as the income derived from spending fifty hours a week away from home! Isn't that reason enough to look diligently for a moneymaking opportunity that can be done at home during flexible hours so as not to detract from the "income" you're already receiving as a full-time homemaker?

A Home Business for the Single Woman

When the term "full-time homemaker" is used many people erroneously assume the title can apply only to a slightly chubby cookie-baking mother who is habitually clad in a red gingham apron. Yet, a homemaker can be anyone—even a single woman or a single man. If you have a place to live and you are the one responsible for its upkeep and "hominess" then you are a homemaker even if your "family" consists only of yourself.

A HOME CAREER FOR A SINGLE WOMAN?

Of course, most single people aren't nearly as interested in home careers as are married women. After all, if you're by yourself most nights and evenings, you likely relish being with people during the day. However, for single persons who do have the desire to stay at home, a home business is just as workable as for married persons. While the care of a husband or of children may not enter into the picture, other factors may make a home business idea quite attractive.

Many unmarried women find themselves left to care for aging parents while married brothers and sisters lead busy lives hundreds of miles away. A home business can be the ideal solution for a single person who must pay a sitter to take care of aging parents while she works at an outside job.

Then, too, handicapped single people often find home careers perfect for their situations. Sadly, the greatest handicap most of these afflicted people have is not their physical disability, but the handicap caused by employers' reluctance to hire them. A home career offers handicapped people the chance for fulfillment, higher self-esteem, a certain degree of independence, and much needed cash. Yet, a home career also offers the flexibility necessary for those whose weakened condition or physical impairments might make eight hours of uninterrupted work impossible. With a home business the handicapped person can work while he feels like it and can rest when the need arises. Since he is his own employer, he also has the option to work as slowly as is comfortable.

WHAT ABOUT THE LONE PARENT?

Due to death or divorce many women are now finding it necessary to not only support themselves with the salary from an outside job, but to raise children on a single paycheck. Unfortunately, the lone parent who works must also bear all those expenses mentioned in Chapter 21. A working mother has to pay out a hefty portion of her earnings for baby-sitting, transportation, and clothes. The monetary pinch is especially difficult for the working single mother who does not have the advantage of a husband's income to compensate for her expenses. Even though the take-home pay is meager, she has no choice about working.

Most mothers who are widowed or divorced struggle along never realizing that a home business could possibly be the right solution to their economic problems. While admittedly, it's terrifying to realize you are solely responsible for the family's food, clothes, and shelter, it's even more terrifying to contemplate starting a home business which might result in days or weeks of no profits whatsoever. For this reason, many single women who do consider the possibility of starting a home business usually put the idea out of their minds with the rationalization that a home business works only for those who don't have to work. Yet, it is possible for the lone parent to start a business by minimizing the risk of facing times with no income.

HOW CAN I GET STARTED?

For the single woman or lone parent, the safest course of action is to begin the home business as a "moonlight" endeavor. Of course, there isn't much moonlight time left over for the woman who must single-handedly be mother and daddy and breadwinner. But if you can possibly find a way to squeeze two or three hours a day from an already full schedule, you can experiment with running a home business. A month or two of moonlighting will give you a fairly good indication of whether or not the business is going to work. Admittedly, those weeks of working an outside job, keeping house, cooking meals, minding children, and at the same time running a home business, are going to be the most hectic and tiring weeks of your life. Nevertheless, if you can survive the schedule long enough to get the business rolling so that the outside job can be given up, you'll know the results were well worth the sacrifice of living with those weeks of the hectic schedule.

PREPARING FOR LEAN TIMES

It's a good idea to try to put aside a few dollars (another extremely difficult task!) before you begin your home business. While you are struggling to get the business going, you may need to have some cash to fall back on for necessary expenses such as rent and utilities. If you can't put aside some cash, don't go full-time until you have something saved up for emergencies. Continue moonlighting and use your moonlighting income to build up savings for the time when you go full-time with the home business.

Another cushion tactic is to sign up with one of the temporary work agencies in your city. These agencies supply part-time or temporary workers to business firms which need extra help during Christmas season or vacation time. There's no fee charged to you. The company for whom you work pays the agency and then you get your paycheck from the agency. Some of the agencies even allow you to take a paid vacation after you achieve a certain number of weeks of work. You don't have to work every time the agency calls you. You can work one week and then go a month before you work another week. This makes the work especially appealing to a woman involved in a home business. While office workers such as secretaries, clerks, and typists are the ones most frequently employed by these agencies, there are also some openings for women without office skills. Some warehouses and stores call the agencies when they need temporary or part-time help. During the summer after my freshman year of college I worked for two agencies: Manpower, Inc. and Kelly Girls, Inc. One of my jobs involved two and a half months of work at a warehouse, where I worked four hours each day. Because of my experiences with the temporary agencies, I learned the value of having easy access to available part-time work. For the woman whose beginning home business might need a slight financial boost, the temporary agencies might be a perfect solution.

WHAT'S WRONG WITH A HOME BUSINESS?

For the mother who is raising her children by herself, every single dollar counts. Accordingly, the lone parent who undertakes a home career may find herself unwittingly falling into a hard to resist dilemma. Since the home businesswoman sets her own hours, she can work as much or as little as she wishes. For most women who are running a home business merely for the pleasure of purchasing "extras" no problem is involved. The married homeworker simply works more when she needs more cash and slacks off when she has other things she'd rather be doing. The lone parent does not have that option. Instead, she may find herself succumbing to the desire for providing more extras and as a consequence she may begin working impossibly long hours. This merely defeats her own purpose. The idea of a home career for the lone parent is to have more time with the children, not less. If the income derived from the home business is not sufficient it would be more advisable to learn cost-cutting measures or to raise prices, or to seek additional outlets for the goods or services. Increasing work time only defeats the purpose of being in business for yourself—flexibility.

CHILDREN AND A HOME BUSINESS

When a lone parent thinks about choosing a potential home career, it's helpful if she can find one in which the children can also participate. Since any working mother who is raising her children alone has more duties than she has time, it's essential that she enlist all the help she can get. While raking leaves or washing dishes may seem appropriate chores to assign to children, most children will feel as if they have contributed more to the running of the household if they can actually participate in the business. To them, making jewelry, chopping nuts, or stuffing rag dolls seems much more grown-up and responsible than does bed-making and dishwashing.

Children who participate in the home business are also much more likely to help you with publicity. You'll be surprised to discover how many contacts an eight-year-old has. If the business is "ours" instead of "mine," he's much more likely to help you spread the word.

WHAT ARE THE REWARDS?

For the lone parent who is already financially burdened and physically tired, a home business might seem like the ultimate "pie in the sky" dream. Yet the enterprising mother, who with her children, finds a way to make her dream into reality will find that the rewards greatly outweigh the disadvantages.

With a home job you have options. For instance, if you want to spend the summer "goofing off" while the children are out of school, you can arrange your schedule in a manner to make this possible. Enlist the children's cooperation and with all of you working hard during the other months of the year a vacation becomes a reality.

While a woman who works at an outside job may find her career advancement possibilities severely limited, the home businesswoman faces no such dead end. Regardless of what occupation you have chosen, your advancement is limited only by your imagination and willingness to work. As long as you're willing to explore all possible avenues of success, you have advancement opportunities waiting for you.

The best part of a home career is that you don't have to work as hard. You may work longer hours or even perform physically harder work, but you'll quite likely discover that the work is not nearly as tiring. There's something about being your own boss that makes any business seem less like toil. And when you're engaged in a chore you enjoy, work is not nearly as exhausting.

23

Job
Ideas

If you haven't come up with some ideas for jobs by now, you must be trying awfully hard *not* to! However, for those who are still pondering, here's a potpourri of ideas for further pondering.

SELLING FOOD ITEMS

What Does It Take?

Of course, the prerequisite to any successful retailing is a quality product. How do you know if your pickles or bread or carrot cake is of superior quality? You don't have to wonder. People have already told you. If you are asked to bring your specialty to every church supper, P.T.A. meeting, or club gathering, then you must be blending your recipe's ingredients in an acceptable manner.

But having a terrific recipe is no guarantee of success with marketing a food item. The product must also be reasonably simple to produce, relatively low in production cost, easily stored and transported, and not excessively fragile. In addition, your gourmet delight must also be able to meet all government specifications and regulations—which are numerous on f~od items.

What Can I Sell?

Almost anything people like to eat *could* be a moneymaker, but some items are really too difficult to produce at home and to market on a part-time basis. Things which must be refrigerated can create problems, too; so unless you really go big time and buy the proper refrigeration equipment, refrigerated items should be ruled out. Another trouble-maker is multi-ingredient wares such as fruit cake. Fruit cake is a good selling item, but it takes so many ingredients—expensive, high quality ingredients—and so much time to chop and prepare them that the profits are hard to come by. Items such as bread, pound cakes, cookies (if they are not too fragile), candies, hors d'oeuvres, and tea time sandwiches are more easily dealt with. Also to be avoided are items which cannot be easily transported. Meringue pies and soft cookies are too much trouble unless you're willing to add the additional expense of securing sturdy boxes.

What Do People Like to Buy?

Appearance sells more food items than taste does. Certainly the product must *taste* good, or the customer won't come back, but first it must *look* good in order to attract attention. It's a mistake to make homemade items look too factory perfect, however. Part of the appeal lies in their uncommercialized look. Particularly, if you sell your wares at craft shows, sales are increased by the old-fashioned look. Customers don't really want to buy a jar of strawberry preserves nearly as badly as they want to evoke memories of grandma and the long gone days of childhood. That's why so many sellers of food wares wear old-fashioned bonnets, cover the table with a red-checked cloth, and tie colorful bows around the tops of pickle jars.

In addition to buying memories, some people like to buy time, and if you're selling food items you also may be selling someone a few minutes of spare time. With more women now working outside their homes than ever before, fewer homemakers have the time to spend in making the kind of foods their families like to eat. Yet most of these homemakers do want to give their families good things to eat. That's where your talent comes into the picture. You can make a dozen brownies for the working mother who gets home at 6:00 p.m. and has to have the brownies at the P.T.A. meeting by 7:30. Because you've taken care of the obligation for her, she can spend her time making a good meal for her family without worrying about getting the brownies made. You've not only sold her a product, you may have sold her a few extra minutes to spend relaxing with her children.

Professional people sometimes need a helping hand, too. Caterers are called upon to furnish all sorts of food items, but many prefer to make only their own speciality and to "farm out" the other assignments. Consequently, if you show up with a wonderful recipe for cheese straws, or a similar snack, you might find yourself becoming a regular supplier. The key to success here is dependability. You *must* arrive on time with the goods you've promised, because not only your income, but the caterers' reputation depends on your ability to consistently deliver a quality product on time.

You might become so proficient as a food salesman as to warrant becoming a caterer yourself. Although catering as a profession requires more information than these few pages can give you, you should be able to get the help you need by contacting a trade school and inquiring about a catering course. If you do not live near a trade school, try contacting one anyway to find out what is used as a textbook. Then, if attending classes is impractical, studying the textbook may be of help to you.

Catering involves much, much more than merely providing food items. To succeed, you'll need to invest in such items as punch bowls, silver candlesticks and trays, and lace tablecloths. Since these items require a considerable cash outlay, you might find it more profitable to begin slowly by becoming a caterer only of limited food wares which would not involve any stock of party paraphernalia. Some hostesses will gladly provide their own silver and tablecloths and would need only sandwiches and canapes from you. This is the kind of catering you can do without becoming too involved in purchasing expensive "props."

What About Decorated Cakes?

Another popular food item is decorated special occasion cakes. Nearly every family will at one time or another need a fancy birthday cake, and if icing artistry is your specialty, you'll have a chance to profit from other families' happy celebrations. If you become very involved in this career, the inventory of pans, color paste, and decorating tips can become quite expensive. However the best part of cake decorating as a career is that you can start small and add to your inventory as the profits begin to come in. A set of round cake pans, a basic set of decorating tips, and a few jars of the most frequently used colors will start you on your way. YWCAs, recreation centers, and even stores offer courses in cake decoration, so learning the techniques should not be a stumbling block.

What About Government Regulations?

The sale of food items carries more limitations than the sale of any other items. Your product will be under the jurisdiction of the Food and Drug Administration, so you must contact this agency to obtain guidelines. Additionally, you must meet regulations imposed by your local health department. You'll have to have a health card as proof that you have no contagious diseases, and you will have to meet certain specifications about your work area. Periodic inspections are made to be certain sanitary conditions are maintained. Call your health department for details about your particular case as rules vary from state to state.

MAIL-ORDER SELLING

Have you ever noticed the tremendous number of classified ads in the back of magazines, offering items to be sold through the mail? Perhaps you have read some of those ads and wondered if you, too, could profitably market a product in a similar way.

Mail-order selling does offer opportunities for a homemaker to make extra money, but like any other business it requires work and persistence. And in addition, it requires an investment in inventory. While most other income opportunities are based on skills or a self-produced stock, mail-order selling requires you to first spend money before making any.

Deciding on a Product

The logical first step is to determine what you're going to sell. The product should be small and light enough to be inexpensively mailed. It should reach the customer in the same good condition it was in when you mailed it. It should be inexpensive enough to be readily affordable. The wholesale cost should be low enough to provide you a reasonable return for the efforts invested in packing, shipping, and record keeping.

A studious inspection of the ads proffered by others in the mail order business will give you an indication of the type of material most successfully sold by mail. Ask your librarian for back issues of magazines to determine if individuals who are placing ads have been doing so for several months or years. If so, apparently those businesses are generating sufficient income to warrant continued advertisement. Make note of the kinds of items offered and the price range of the items. This will give you some indication of what consumers will buy, sight unseen, through the mail. The price ranges in the ads will give you an idea of the maximums and minimums which are feasible. Also, try to analyze your intended product as though *you* were the customer. Would you buy such an item through the mail from an individual you did not know?

It's not a good idea to try selling wearing apparel which depends on an exact fit. Of course, it can be done—Sears does it all the time—but you have neither the staff nor the finances of Sears, so wearing apparel may be more trouble than it is worth. Remember, too, that it's standard procedure for mail order businesses to offer money-back guarantees on all goods and clothing is more likely to come back than is any other product.

Another area many mail-order sellers avoid is the sale of holiday related material. However, for the homemaker who wishes to work only a few months of the year, holiday sales might prove workable. Just be *very* sure your "leftovers" will be just as salable next year as they are this year. Also, timing your advertising is critical when dealing with seasonal products. A January ad for Christmas items will generate no sales. The November issue of most publications comes on the newsstands toward the last of October, so this is just about the latest date you can advertise, because you'll need to allow at least six weeks for the product to be processed and shipped to the customer. Bear in mind, too, that magazines work far in advance of the date on the cover. Many publications have their December issue finished by the first of June, so get that ad in early.

Obtaining the Product

How does the would-be mail-order entrepreneur obtain a product to sell? She locates a wholesaler. This can be done by consulting a book such as *The Thomas Register of American Manufacturers* at your library. After you find out who manufactures the product you need, write to the company and find out if they will sell directly to you or if they will give you the name of their distributor. This works if you know the name of the company which manufactures what you need. If you don't know the manufacturer of the product you are seeking, look through the specialized magazines to find a supplier. Publications such as *Souvenirs and Novelties, Profitable Craft Merchandising,* and *Toys and Games* will probably have the information you require.

Getting a Mailing List

The yellow pages contain listings of companies which sell mailing lists. In addition, specialized magazines such as *Direct Mail Advertising* carry ads from companies called list brokers. These list brokers will supply you with names and addresses of prospective customers. Seeing the names of some of the companies who rent lists may surprise you. Practically every organization or merchandiser who deals in anything through the mail will offer its lists to other mail-order companies. Magazines even sell their subscription lists.

You can buy lists which are broken down by categories—lists of housewives, executives, farmers, or previous mail-order buyers. Buy carefully and selectively. A mailing list firm should be able to guarantee that a reasonably high percentage of the addresses are current.

The best mailing list is the one you make up yourself from previous customers. As your business grows, profits can be increased as you gradually weed out the "dead" listings and replace them with "live" ones to whom you've previously sold goods.

Advertising

Advertising is the most expensive part of the mail-order business. Even a tiny ad in the back of a nationally circulated magazine may run as much as three or four dollars per word. Additionally, some magazines require that you purchase a minimum of three months space at one time. You may pay as much as a hundred dollars for a ten-word "bare bones" ad. (You probably can't get by with ten words, because your address will use up at least five.)

Besides the classifieds, some mail-order advertisers also use display advertising. This is the kind which is done in columns or blocks on either side of the reading material. Display advertising is extremely expensive. Send an 8″ × 10″ glossy of your product if you use a display ad. An ad covering only an eighth of a page may cost more than three hundred dollars for one insertion.

Because advertising is so expensive, you'll want to word your ad concisely and descriptively, and place it where it will do the most good. If you're selling quilt patterns, put the ad in a publication such as *Quilt World* or *Quilter's Newsletter*. If you're selling dried fruit, place your ad in a magazine such as *The Mother Earth News* or *Backpacker*.

REFUNDING

What Is It?

Refunding as a home moneymaker is generally overlooked. It is the process of using coupons, package labels, and forms to obtain money back on goods you have purchased. While most homemakers have occasionally used those "cents off" coupons found in magazines and newspapers, most look on refunding as a part-time money-saving measure and not as a genuine moneymaking career. Yet, money *can* be made with refunding and the money isn't nickels and dimes either. For the refunder who is motivated and organized the reward is hundreds of dollars a year.

144

What Does It Take?

The essential ingredient in refunding is constant dedication along with a conviction that refunding really does work. Too many homemakers refuse to believe so simple a moneymaking effort can truly put dollars in their purses.

"Why would companies want to give away money?" most nonrefunders ask in bewilderment. "There must be some kind of catch to it."

The manufacturers' motivation is purely mercenary. Large manufacturing companies are willing to gamble a quarter or even a dollar on the quality of their products. It's worth it to them to invest a small refund on the chance of having you like their product so much that you will develop a life-long loyalty to it. To them a one-time one dollar refund will theoretically be offset thousands of times in the future when you buy their product over and over again.

However, the "pro" refunder immediately disappoints her benefactor. The "pro" never develops a passion for any name brand. Her loyalty is to the label which is currently carrying the highest refund offer.

How Do I Get Started?

1. Look for refunds. Initially, you'll find most of your refunds in your local newspaper. Most daily newspapers have one issue per week which carries detailed food ads. Perhaps you're already using some of the cents off coupons but have bypassed the real money in refunds.

"But is it really worth it?" you ask. "By the time I pay postage, I won't really have anything left to show for my effort."

The manufacturers, like you, realize that postage takes a bite out of your refund, so most refund offers are adjusted upward to compensate for postage costs. Several years ago when I first started refunding, refund offers of twenty-five cents were common. Now you seldom see any for less than a dollar. Still, while postage costs have increased, refund offers have become even more numerous. How can you tell if the money is worth the effort? The refund should be adequate to compensate you for your postage and give you at least the price of two additional stamps or it is not even worth putting into the envelope.

A good source of refund information is the grocery store.

Have you noticed those pads attached to the counters near certain products? Often the forms offer refunds in exchange for a required number of labels.

Another source of refund information is the package itself. Numerous vegetables, cereals, or even deodorants have a money-back offer on the back or side of the package.

The most complete source of refunding information is found in the refunding magazines and newspapers. These are publications which tell you which offers are currently in effect and what must be sent in to get your refund. If you intend to get really serious about refunding, you'll need to subscribe to at least one refund bulletin. The cost of the subscription will be more than offset by the money you take in. In addition to "cash backs" (the refunders' term for the actual money refunds) the bulletins list other refunding delights. Certain products occasionally have offers such as "mail five boxtops and $1.00 and get a cake plate valued at $4.98." These offerings make money for the refunders, so the bulletins list these kinds of deals, too.

There are numerous bulletins available. However, before subscribing to any, write for a sample copy. Most will send you one for a small fee. Look over the bulletins and subscribe to the one which seems to best meet your needs.

A really good bulletin is one that carries information in clear terms, lists practically all current refunding offers, and most important of all, gets to you on time. A bulletin does no good if it arrives after the refund's time limit expires. If you hesitate to pay money for the refunding bulletin, do what many of the frequent users do: contribute refunding information to the editor and get financial rewards for that, too!

There are a number of good bulletins, but I particularly like *Golden Opportunities* which is edited by Carole Kratz. The address is Box 262, Hannibal, OH 43931. In addition to bulletins, Mrs. Kratz also offers books which explain refunding in detail and may be helpful to the beginner. Since prices change, it's best to write, enclose a stamped, self-addressed envelope, and wait for a reply before sending money for a sample copy.

2. *Collect the required labels.* The novice refunder usually gets bogged down in disappointment when she realizes she has to spend money to get the necessary labels. Of course, buying all those needed products at one time would be expensive, but the seasoned refunder doesn't do business that way at all. After you do refunding for a while you learn which companies are

likely to give refunds and which ones never do. You learn to save labels even when there is no refund offer going on. Then when something is offered, you don't have to rush out and buy that product, because you already have the required label in your files.

3. *Follow the rules.* It is a waste of time and postage if you don't follow the manufacturers' rules for obtaining the refund. If the form says "box bottom" send the bottom, not the top. If the form says "form required" send the form. (Some companies say "form required" and then don't hold you to this. The refunding bulletins tell you which companies will send you the cash without the refund form. However, unless you have this verification from a dependable bulletin, it is a waste of postage to try to get the refund without the form.)

4. *Keep accurate records.* A good filing system is essential. Your labels should be organized to allow instant access. Your mailing record should be kept up to date so you can readily determine which refunds have arrived and which ones have not. Most refund offers specify "one to a household" so don't waste a stamp and embarrass yourself by having poor records which end up cheating you out of a refund.

5. *Make friends with other refunders.* One of the rewards of refunding is the friendships you'll make. Each issue of the refunding bulletins carries ads from other refunders who will gladly swap information and required forms with you.

6. *Learn to be a smart shopper.* Refunding is fun, but don't let your enthusiasm override your good sense. Nothing is a bargain if your family tosses it into the garbage. Buy only what you can use.

Learn to work sales, cents off coupons, and refunding as a profitable trio. For instance, I once had a cents off coupon which I had been holding for several months. The item involved was a high priced convenience food so I felt that it was not a bargain, even with the coupon. Eventually I saw another coupon in the paper which offered a mail-in refund for the same product. I carefully hoarded that goody, too. Finally patience paid off. One week in the grocery ads I noticed the item offered for sale as one of the store's specials. Between the sale price and cents off coupon I got the item practically free of charge. Then I cut off the label, sent in the required form and got a worthwhile refund on a product which had cost me next to nothing!

WRITING

What Does It Take?

For the woman with limited household space, a writing career offers about as much flexibility as anyone could wish. A space four feet by four feet can be your office. Writing requires little equipment. A typewriter, even an antique, secondhand manual one, and a good dictionary are about all you'll need in the beginning. Writing doesn't require a tremendous amount of education either. Most aspiring writers don't realize it, but if they got as far as the tenth grade and paid close attention in English class, they probably have the language skills necessary for some writing. (Many famous writers had even less education than that, but they compensated with a certain amount of natural talent and a voracious consumption of all the reading matter they could get.) A writing career isn't limited by age, sex, or occupation. Editors don't care if you are a Martian ditch digger. All they want is good material.

How Can a Homemaker Become a Writer?

The first requirement is so obvious it sounds ridiculous, but it's the step most easily ignored by Pulitzer Prize aspirants. You can't be a writer unless you write! Becoming a writer isn't as simple as becoming a basketweaver. If you want to be a basketweaver, you think about it for a while and then you get up and go weave baskets. Not so with writing. Too many talented people think about writing, dream about writing, even mentally compose writing, and then follow up by *never* going near a typewriter. If you want to write, don't just think about it—*do it!*

How Can a Beginner Get Started?

The first step is to go to the library and get a copy of the most current edition of *The Writer's Market*. Choose a publication which carries the kind of articles you like to read, then look to see what the magazine's editorial policy is. Beginners are usually more successful with the magazines with smaller circulation figures and smaller writer's paychecks. The more prestigious the magazine or the more it pays the more competition you'll have from experienced professionals. Naturally, everybody wants to write for *Reader's Digest* and *National Geographic,* but for a beginner that's aiming a bit high. However, occasionally it has happened that a beginner made a big sale the first time.

Before writing, ask the librarian for at least a year's back issues of your chosen publication. Study each issue intently. Reading is not the same as study. Analyze the articles to see what they have in common. Study opening paragraphs to learn what "hook" attracts the reader's attention. Note the way the authors smooth the writing with varying sentence length, transitional phrases, active verbs, and colorful descriptions.

After studying the magazine until you know it forward and backward, write to the editor and ask for the editorial guidelines. Type your request neatly and enclose a stamped, self-addressed envelope. Editorial guidelines tell you exactly how magazine editors want their submissions prepared. Some outline acceptable subject matter for you. Most tell you the form to use in typing the manuscript. And usually the guidelines will tell you the current pay scale.

After reading the guidelines, notice whether the magazine will accept unsolicited manuscripts. Most of the lower paying magazines do accept unsolicited manuscripts, but some prefer a query letter instead. A query letter is one which you write to an editor, giving him your idea for a possible article and asking him for permission to send it on speculation (you are willing to write it on the chance that he might like it, but if he does not, he has no obligation to pay you anything). Queries save time for writers and editors, so many magazines and writers prefer to do business that way.

After you've written your story and rewritten it and polished it and repolished it, type it neatly according to those editorial guidelines, enclose a stamped, self-addressed envelope, and *put it in the mail.* I've never yet encountered an editor who goes around checking closets and drawers for possible manuscripts.

Small magazines have small staffs, so don't expect to hear from them in less than three months. Meanwhile, read *Writer's Digest* every month and write more manuscripts and mail them.

Writer's Digest is a monthly magazine for writers. It gives technical help as well as inspirational help and market information. The address is 9933 Alliance Road, Cincinnati, OH 45242.

Writing is an extremely satisfying way to fulfill your creative urges. It's also an effective way to share your Christian faith. One article in a magazine with a circulation of a million or even a quarter million will reach more people than you'll ever be able to personally reach with your testimony in an entire lifetime. The paychecks you receive will not be as thrilling to you as will the letters you receive from readers whose lives have been influenced by what you wrote.

One last word about writing. If anyone asks if you are employed, tell them you are a writer. No one will take you seriously if you don't take yourself seriously. You don't have to sell anything to be a writer, just as you don't have to sell any baskets to call yourself a basket weaver. All you have to do is work at it.

24

Women
Who
Do

GAYLE MCGRATH, SCRIMSHANDER

Gayle McGrath of Fort Myers, Florida, is a young wife and mother with a home business that's really different. While Gayle's income comes from a business she conducts at home, the location of home varies from week to week. The McGraths have taken Gayle's successful home business and have put it on wheels. Gayle, her husband Kevin, and their three-year-old-son Kevie, live in a motor home while the McGraths travel about the country setting up shop at various fairs, craft shows, and horse shows.

Gayle is a scrimshander—one who carves on ivory. While most people think of bearded old sea captains when the word *scrimshander* is mentioned, Gayle's proficiency at her work dispels all doubt that "lady" and "scrimshander" are compatible words.

Scrimshaw is an ancient art, but the height of its popularity came during the days of the whaling ships. While that era is long past, the art form it created remains as intriguing as ever.

Scrimshaw is made by using a sharp pointed tool to scratch lines into pieces of ivory. Then the scratches are inked with India ink and the scene stands out in vivid detail. Although scrimshaw was originally done on whale's teeth, elephant ivory is the medium for today's art because whales are on the endangered species list and whale ivory is no longer available.

Gayle McGrath's career as a scrimshander began as a hobby and blossomed into a business after her son was born. Not wanting to return to her old job, Gayle looked about for other ways to bring in income without leaving her baby with baby sitters.

"I was a commercial artist before my son was born," Gayle says. "Consequently, I'd had quite a bit of training in art. Then one day my mother-in-law brought home some scrimshaw—which I'd never seen before—and I fell in love with it. I said, 'I've just got to do some of that!'"

Gayle's art training was far removed from scrimshaw. She had done graphic production and design and had worked in a studio which handled advertising accounts. Yet, she feels her background in art did enable her to learn scrimshaw more easily than might have been the case if she had not had previous training.

"I started out loving scrimshaw and wanting to do it," she relates. "Initially, it was only a hobby. Then it became a weekend thing. We would go to a weekend show and the whole family was together and we had a lot of fun with it. Now we travel full time."

"Before Kevie was born, I worked full time," Gayle continues. "After he was born I was eager to get back into doing art, but I didn't want to leave Kevie alone with a sitter. Scrimshaw has allowed me to be both a full-time mother and a full-time artist."

Gayle's scrimshaw started out as her home business, but now the project has grown to be a family activity. Gayle does all the art work and her husband, Kevin, is the salesman.

"I'm strictly the artist and my husband is strictly the salesman," she says with a laugh. "It doesn't bother me to talk to people, but I'm just not the salesperson type at all. I'd much rather make scrimshaw than sell it. I enjoy talking, too—but just don't make me sell anything!"

The McGraths have covered quite a bit of territory since

beginning their business venture, and Gayle feels the experience has been good for all of them.

"We do a little bit of everything," she says. "We've done arts and crafts shows—a lot of those—as well as state and county fairs and horse shows. We really enjoy the traveling. Kevie especially loves the horse shows and the fairs. Once we were parked next to a clown at one of the fairs and Goofo the clown was our neighbor that week. This is really a wonderful way for a child to grow up. We've been in situations where the high-wire performers had their motor home on one side of us and the owners of the dog act were parked behind us. It's really been an experience for all of us. We look at it as an education."

Gayle's work has branched out in several directions since the family hit the road. Now she not only makes scrimshaw but also repairs pieces people bring to her. Some old pieces do not have deep enough grooves, and the ink has worn off. Gayle cuts the scratches deeper and applies a new coat of ink.

Gayle does not mind competition from other scrimshanders. She welcomes the growth of the popularity of scrimshaw because she feels that in this way the quality of the craft will be increased when the field becomes more competitive. She's distressed to see work which she calls "hen scratching" and feels that the more scrimshanders there are the more discriminating customers will be.

Gayle's design ideas come from various places. Although she originally began her career with the traditional nautical motifs, she now creates custom designs and lets her customers dream up what they want. She does a large number of horses, but she's also had requests for such things as a tractor-trailer, an organ grinder and monkey, and even such things as steam engines and motorcycle emblems.

"When the customers find out I'll do custom work, they let their imaginations run wild," she laughs. "I just never know what they are going to come up with for me to draw!"

Gayle has found that creating scrimshaw for money changes the creator's perspective considerably.

"You become much more eager to please," she says. "Initially, I intended to do nautical scenes only because that's the way it 'should' be, and I was going to stick to my guns on that point. Then somebody came up and asked for custom work—an eighteen wheeler or something like that, and I said, 'Aw, why not? We've got to eat tonight!' Now I do eighteen wheelers or whatever else the customer wants."

Being a full-time artist is comparable in many ways to holding down any other full-time job. Gayle feels that any job has unappealing aspects at times and that it would be unrealistic to expect the situation to be otherwise. However, she insists that most of the time her work is thoroughly enjoyable. Being a full-time mother more than compensates for any difficulties involved in being a full-time artist, too. She even feels her son has been highly adaptable to the unusual circumstances of his home life.

The McGraths are having so much fun with their traveling home business that they have no plans to change their lifestyle until Kevie is old enough for school.

"This is a permanent thing for us," Gayle says. "I'm sure we'll travel until he starts school and after that, I'll still figure out some way to do scrimshaw. I really do enjoy it."

GLADYS WYAS, QUILTER

Gladys Wyas of Saint Charles, Missouri, has found a unique service job which has enabled her to have her own business without leaving home. Gladys has capitalized on the revived interest in quilt-making by offering a quilting service for those who enjoy making quilt tops but do not want to involve themselves in the actual quilting required to finish the project.

Gladys' service job is a perfect example of a service which can be done as an aid to people who for one reason or another find it either inconvenient or distasteful to do the task for themselves.

While many homeworkers become involved in a business as a natural outgrowth of a beloved hobby, this was not true in Gladys' case. She had given considerable thought to the possibility of finding a lucrative home business. Because Gladys is a quilt-maker herself she realized that while many women love the piecing and applique work involved in making quilt tops, a great many women do not care for the actual quilting, which is the final step. After giving the matter consideration Gladys came to the conclusion that quilting for others would be the perfect home business for her.

Like most service jobs, a quilting business requires an initial investment in equipment. In Gladys' case the machine she needed, plus the thread and frames, cost a thousand dollars. Like most homemakers, Gladys was not able to walk into a store and plunk down that much money in order to go into business. But rather than go into debt, she found a way to finance her own business plans.

"This was not a hobby turned business," she says. "I baby-sat for others while my children were smaller. I saved the baby-sitting money and bought the quilting equipment with the idea of starting a business."

For Gladys' service job, the "where to put it" problem was of prime importance. The equipment used for machine quilting requires a considerable amount of operating space. The quilting frames were attached to the ceiling and run on a track. Because the frames move back and forth as the quilting is done, it is necessary to have a room at least twenty-four feet long. Gladys uses a portion of her basement as her special place.

Like most women who begin a business at home, Gladys puts her family first. She has five children and readily admits that raising her family takes precedence over any moneymaking activity. Yet, her children and her husband are proud of her financial accomplishments and contribute a great deal to her success.

"My family comes first," Gladys says, "and they all help a lot. My fifteen-year-old son and my seventeen-year-old daughter help me roll in the dacron batting and take out the finished quilt. The little boys, ages eleven and seven, help carry things downstairs for me, and they do a lot of other little necessary things, too. Believe it or not, they even do a lot of advertising for me!"

Gladys does have one business problem which has been difficult to cope with in spite of the cooperative attitude of her entire family. Her husband doesn't work "normal" hours.

"My husband works from 3:30 p.m. until 12:30 a.m.," she says. "That means a breakfast for him at 9:00 and a big meal at 1:00 p.m. Consequently, my working time is really split up during the day. In fact, I do most of my work in the evenings. If my husband worked during the daytime, I believe I could do twice as many quilts and could make twice as much money with the business."

Still, Gladys admits that the income she has derived from her business has been considerable for a homeworker who must run her business on such a fragmented working schedule. In 1977 she did two hundred quilts and by September, 1978, she had increased her production by 50 percent.

"I charge by the size of the quilt," she says. "However, when I calculated my income according to the actual hours I worked, the salary varied from three to six dollars per hour. That's more than minimum wage, and many women don't make that much by going out to a job every day. Actually, if it became necessary I could go into business in a bigger way and I could make more. I could also sell quilts—either my own or other people's—on consignment. I could advertise or even go to craft shows. However, at the present I don't want to do these things."

Gladys has one vital bit of information to pass along to others who might be thinking about going into any kind of service business. "Be sure you know what you are doing in any business *before* you advertise," she emphasizes. "Build up your business slowly and you'll be a lot more relaxed about it and will enjoy it more."

"I know someone who began a business before she had even tried to do it for herself," Gladys continues. "She really had herself in a mess! That's like jumping into the deep end of a pool and not knowing how to swim!"

Of course, Gladys follows her own advice. Her quilting business was built slowly and cautiously. "I had several tops of my own that needed quilting," she says. "I practiced on my own and then on some that belonged to some of my relatives. After that, I let out the word that I was in business. Word just spread and my business kept increasing. I have never advertised," she says. "If you do good work, word of mouth is your best advertising."

Gladys is enthusiastic on the subject of her home business. For her, a career has combined admirably well with motherhood and its responsibilities. "My five children are my number-one job," Gladys says, "but I really do enjoy working at home, too. With a home business I can run downstairs and work for thirty minutes between trips to the school, to scout meetings, and other things like that. This is the only kind of job I could have right now."

Gladys has also found that running a home business is easier for her because her husband supports her in her decision to be a businesswoman. His agreement and cooperation make her moneymaking project much easier for her.

"With my husband's working hours, he is not at home much while I am working," she says, "but he does drive for me when we need to go to downtown St. Louis for supplies or to pick up quilts from older ladies who do not drive. That helps me out considerably. However, the biggest help he contributes is by not complaining because I don't keep the house as clean as I used to!'"

LOUISE TUGGLE, CREATOR OF SHELL JEWELRY

Louise Tuggle of Sanibel Island, Florida, has a home business which came into existence because Louise could not bear the thought of seeing something as beautiful as a sea shell go to waste.

Louise and her husband, Jason, have a home on Sanibel Island, which is one of the most famous shelling beaches in the world. Because the beach is so near their house, the Tuggles find it quite natural to spend innumerable hours strolling on the beach. Inevitably, too, the infinite variety of shells make it hard to resist gathering handfuls of the beautiful specimens. Such delights as the sailor's ear shell, the banded tulip shell, the turkey wing shell, and even the rare junonia shell are available on Sanibel Island.

"I had boxes and boxes of shells," she remembers, "so I decided to design a necklace for myself."

Of course, that first experimental necklace was only the beginning. With so much raw material to choose from, Louise could hardly be blamed for creating more and more of the beautiful ornaments. However, her work was for love, not money. The idea of selling the necklaces did not occur to her immediately. "Sometimes I would be in a shopping center or some other public place," Louise recalls, "and a stranger would rush up to me and say, 'Oh, where did you get that necklace? I would just love to have one like it myself.'"

Louise's husband, Jason, has enjoyed working with the seashells, too. Since the Tuggles have no small children, they do have more spare time than do couples whose children are still at home. Jason has an extremely demanding job and the hobby Louise has discovered appeals to him as a method of unwinding after a day's work.

"Working on the shells helps him to relax," Louise says. "He does the mechanics, such as drilling the holes in the shells, and I do the fun part—the designing."

After the Tuggles became thoroughly immersed in their new hobby, it seemed only logical for them to sell some of their wares. Consequently, they began participating in local craft shows and discovered that shell jewelry is highly salable.

As a result of the demand for Louise's work, she began to branch out into finding new ways to use her shells. Now her display table carries not only the original jewelry with which she began her business, but also carries exquisite shell-framed mirrors and sophisticated shell-filled ginger jar lamps.

Yet, regardless of what Louise is making, all her creations have one thing in common. Louise does not allow the design as a whole to detract from the elegant simplicity of the shells. "Each shell is beautiful on its own merits," she says. "The simplicity of the shell is the most beautiful part of it for me."

Louise's work is modestly priced considering the labor which goes into each creation. Her small ginger jar lamp is thirty-five dollars and the larger one is sixty dollars. Similar items in exclusive stores sell for twice that much. But Louise insists that the prices she charges are quite acceptable to her. Her real pleasure lies in the designing and creating of her wares, and, as far as she is concerned, making money from them is secondary.

"I want this to always be a fun thing for me," Louise says. "If you become *too* business minded it takes all the fun out of a craft, and more than anything else this is a nice hobby. Working with shells has truly been both a job and a pleasure for me."

LOIS COLLINS, TUTOR

Lois Collins, of Forest Park, Georgia, began teaching school in 1968. Since then she has "retired" to full-time homemaking and motherhood, but she still uses her teaching skills tutoring children who need more help than they are receiving at school.

Although Lois does have a teaching degree, she is quick to point out that a degree in teaching is not a mandatory prerequisite to becoming a successful tutor. "Absolutely anyone can tutor if she knows the material," Lois says. "You don't even need to have teacher certification. All you need is a place to teach, a working knowledge of your subject and an enthusiasm for your work."

Lois prefers group teaching and recommends this manner as long as no more than five or six students are in the class. For a group situation, Lois charges six dollars per student per hour. Of course, she occasionally encounters children who desperately need help but who are unable to pay. In situations like this, she will put one non-payer into a group with five paying students.

In spite of Lois' success as a tutor, it seems at times that she is mainly interested in working herself out of a job. "If I have a class where the students have a good self-image, I require the mothers to come to class, too," Lois says. "In any teaching situation, the main thing children need is repetition. No mother need pay a tutor for work she can do herself. Therefore, I simultaneously tutor the mother and the child in order that the mother can go home and work with her child herself."

Lois has some very definite ideas on the proper manner for conducting a class. "The most important thing," she says, "is to remember to have fun and to laugh a lot. Don't take the whole thing too seriously. This is necessary because the children have already experienced failure—otherwise they wouldn't need tutoring in the first place. Remember they may have a bad self-image, and you must first teach them to believe they can learn. Praise is a vital classroom element."

Lois prefers to tutor students from the primary grades because she feels those students are easier to teach. They have not been exposed to as many confusing teaching methods as have older children. "I've found that mixing grade levels can work well, too," Lois says. "I let the older children sit at the back of the classroom, and while I'm working with the younger children the older ones will absorb what I'm saying even though they think they are not in on that lesson but are merely sitting back and listening. However, if the students are physically handicapped or are retarded or have a bad self-image, I prefer to work with them individually."

Some parents who bring children to Lois are stunned by her approach. Lois is interested in the total aspect of each child's life and not simply in his classroom presence. "The reason a lot of children can't learn is because of food allergies or malnutrition," she says. "I ask the parents to eliminate tea, coffee, colas, white bread, and sugar from the children's diets while I am teaching them. Children need lots of protein, and they should have their meals on a regular schedule. No child can learn effectively if he must stop reading long enough to worry about whether or not mama's going to cook a meal for him."

Lois feels some would-be tutors don't start a class because they feel they have no suitable place in which to work. But this problem, she says, is the easiest one to overcome. "I have conducted classes in all kinds of places—in my living room, in my church's basement, under a shady tree, or in a child's bedroom—anywhere you can meet together without having it look too much like a classroom," she says.

"Try to explain facts in carefree, lots of fun terms, using common everyday examples," Lois advises. "Don't try to sound too teacherish. Don't make the child feel his entire life depends on the class either. Never quote his previous teachers or in any way remind him of past failures."

Lois feels that the tools necessary for teaching are quite minimal and ingenuity can substitute for a cash investment in teaching aids. "A piece of posterboard can be used in place of a blackboard," she says. "A clipboard or a typewriting tablet can be used, too; anything you can write on works well. Mostly, you'll need a big smile, a lot of love, and the determination that you are going to make each child feel as if he's one of the smartest people in the world."

Lois finds it easier if all students come from the same school district. The reason for this is because of the numerous types of curriculum being used. Each book company has its own method of presenting facts, and changing curriculum confuses children. "I always start with the basics," Lois says. "I let them learn the language and expressions of the curriculum first and then they know what I'm talking about."

Occasionally, Lois has students who require more individualized attention. For those students, Lois will go to the child's home and will teach on a one-to-one basis. The fee she recommends for this is $12.50 per hour.

"When I teach in a home, I prefer to use the child's bedroom as the classroom," she says. "That is already his private domain, and he feels more secure there."

Lois feels that the biggest problem a tutor will encounter is coping with bad self-images of both parents and children. "Schools sometimes shut out parents," she says. "Mothers are made to feel they don't have sense enough to raise children or

160

to tutor them when the need arises. If I can bring mama into the teaching situation she begins to feel more secure. Having mama feel secure causes her to make Johnny feel secure. Johnny learns. Mama's happy. I'm out of a job. However, I'm not worried about that. There are thousands of children out there waiting for the right tutor to come along. I've got more work than I can possibly do anyway."

"Tutoring is a perfect job for homemakers," Lois continues. "College is not necessary—mostly what you get there is terms and philosophy. What we really need are mothers who are willing to teach what they know and who want to build children's self-confidence. A mother with a confident self-image will do a child more good than will a highly educated Ph.D. who might not care nearly as much about that child."

"Unless there's a physical or mental handicap," Lois says, "the only reason Johnny can't learn is because he hasn't been motivated. Johnny gets his self-image from what mama and daddy think of him, and constant nagging without enforcement convinces him he can't learn. That's the main obstacle a tutor has to overcome."

For homemakers who are seriously considering a career as a tutor, Lois has one final word of advice:

"Eat good food, get plenty of rest, and above all be happy. You're going to need all these advantages because you are going to successfully undo all the damage which has been done to so many children."

25

Why Am I Telling You?

It always seemed to me that anyone who sets out to write a how-to book has an obligation to show the readers what makes the writer think he or she is qualified to give advice. I haven't achieved the status of "expert" on any subject, but I do believe I have ideas worth sharing with other homemakers who want to stay home with their children in spite of the pinch of inflation. I am not writing on the basis of theory. I have successfully conducted home businesses, and I believe you can do it, too—if you have the motivation.

My reason for wanting to be a stay-at-home mother comes from my childhood. As long as I can remember, my mother worked, not by choice but by necessity. All through my growing-up years both of us clung to the dream that someday she would be able to quit work and stay home with me. As I look back on those years and remember all the good food she cooked, the beautiful dresses she made, the clean house she kept, and the way she always found time to attend activities I took part in, I also remember there were times when she stayed up all night in order to get everything done. Being a working mother was not just an end of a cherished dream, but was also a severe physical hardship.

As I grew up I determined that someday when I had children I would find a way to stay at home with them. I intended to accomplish this feat by marrying a rich man, but in childish fashion I didn't realize that love is blind to bank balances.

Randal and I had been married three years when Karen was born in 1968. Until the day of her birth I worked and was totally content as a career woman. I was a supervisor in the trust department of a large bank and I truly loved my work. In fact, I loved it so much that I hadn't yet resigned from my job when Karen was born one snowy Sunday afternoon. For a long time after that friends teased me about being so dedicated to work that I couldn't take time off to have a baby.

Like most new mothers, I had postnatal depression, but my tears were for a specific reason. Everytime I looked at Karen I dreaded the time when I must leave her and go back to work. Yet, everytime we looked at our bank balance it seemed I had no choice. I couldn't even enjoy my six-week leave of absence for worrying about leaving her.

When my leave of absence was ended, I reluctantly prepared to return to the business world. Randal, whose mother had always been a full-time homemaker, had a hard time coping with the idea of leaving Karen with a baby sitter. Eventually, he came up with a plan. We would draw a small sum of money from our meager savings account and use the money to supplement his income so that I might stay with Karen a few more weeks.

Of course, since we were young, had been married only three years, and were in the process of buying a home, we were not the world's best money managers. Nevertheless, we dedicated ourselves to learning the art of scrimping. We gave up such luxuries as entertainment, soft drinks, and fresh bread. Instead we watched television, frequented the day-old bread store, and learned ninety-seven ways to fix hamburger.

Our savings account was small and the money ran out when Karen was three months old. Thinking about leaving her upset me so badly, I became ill. I was rushed to the hospital with severe chest pains, and I stayed there for two weeks. There's a strange thing about hospitals: you can't sleep or watch television because of the noise, but you certainly can think.

I prayed over and over that God would somehow make a way

for me to stay at home with my baby. I begged the Lord to please, please allow me the luxury of calling myself "just a housewife."

Back at home, I devoted myself to stretching the few dollars we had. Still, they didn't stretch quite far enough.

Some people might say the solution to my problem came about by accident. But I believe God worked out my problem for me. A very dear friend of mine had decided to go back to work and asked if I would baby-sit her ten-month-old baby. (By this time Karen was fourteen months old.) I felt like one of those cartoons where the picture of a light bulb is drawn over someone's head to suggest a bright idea. It had not previously occurred to me that I could make money at home.

That first home business was on rather an elementary level. After all, most women at one time or another baby-sit for a little extra money, so the idea wasn't too revolutionary. But the job did teach me two important things: God answers prayer, and money can be made without leaving home.

I really didn't enjoy baby-sitting. Corralling two toddlers in diapers is not my idea of fun, but I was glad for the money. However, the job didn't last long. My friend couldn't bear being away from her baby, so she stopped working and found a typing job she could do at home. Dear friend that she was, she also put in a good word for me. Soon I was merrily banging away at my typewriter. The pay was low and the work was boring, but at least those envelopes didn't have to be fed and diapered! That job lasted only a few months, but by that time Karen's second birthday was approaching, and I was determined to continue staying home with her.

I decided to learn to sew because I figured I could save enough on clothes to offset the need to go to work. To my surprise sewing was fun. I enjoyed it so much that I began to make everything imaginable—clothes and lingerie for myself, suits for Randal, everything for Karen, curtains, and even stuffed animals and dolls. My sister-in-law told a store owner about some of the toys I had made and the shopkeeper asked to sell some of my rag dolls on consignment. Once again, I had "fallen" into a job.

I didn't get rich from that endeavor, but I learned a great deal about managing a home business. Also, in the process I accumulated a large box of fabric scraps. When my doll making career ended (I couldn't stand the sight of another rag doll!), I began using the scraps to make doll clothes for Karen's Barbie dolls. Soon I found myself in the business of selling doll clothes. This was really enjoyable but it lasted only a few months. By that time the imported doll clothes began to flood the market, and I could not compete with their low prices.

During the early part of the 1970s garage sales were becoming quite popular. My neighbor and I held our first sale, and it was so successful that all we could do was gape in amazement at the fistfuls of money we had accumulated. Garage sales must be the road to riches, we thought. What if we recruited about ten people to go in with us and then we could keep moving the weekend garage sales from house to house so that even those with only a handful of things to sell could make a profit? We tried this for a while and it worked well until eventually most of us were rid of our junk.

Then one day my cousin asked if I would be willing to conduct a garage sale for him. He wanted the money but he just didn't want the hassle involved in holding the sale. I agreed and started my new career. I discovered that quite a few people like the money from a garage sale but don't like to be bothered with the selling part. The first sale I held on a commission basis netted me $180 for one day's work! I was all set to go into that career full time when our city council passed a law limiting garage sales, requiring permits, etc. There went my big plans.

All the while I was working on my nickel and dime businesses, Randal had been getting occasional raises at work. With conscientious penny pinching, we could live on his salary, but there was no money left over for extras.

Again, a friend came to the rescue. She made beautiful crocheted jewelry, but she hated to sew. When I offered to buy some of her jewelry to use as Christmas presents, she suggested I sew for her as payment. I made her a dress. Another friend heard about it and asked if I would sew for her, too. I was in business again!

I put an ad in the paper offering my sewing services. One call came from a fabric store. Someone was needed to make model garments to be hung throughout the store as advertisement for the fabric. I also received several other calls, and soon I had all the business I could handle. Bags and bags of fabrics and patterns were piled up in my sewing room. I had so many customers that each one had to wait about six weeks to receive her finished garment.

After two years, I had to give up my sewing business. It was *too* successful! Actually, it wasn't the sewing that was nerve-racking, but the customers. Most of them had total disregard for my family and thought nothing of barging in unannounced during our dinner or our favorite television show. My husband put his foot down and announced that my career as a dressmaker was over.

With all the penny-pinching ways I had learned, along with the raises Randal had received, I discovered our finances were in better shape. However, there were those little extras nagging away at me again. We had Karen in a Christian school and that was a drain on our budget. Also, Karen was begging to have music lessons. There seemed to be only one solution—I would go back to work.

Any homemaker who has ever tried to re-enter the job market can probably guess what happened next. The working world was not really glad to have me return, and I found no welcoming open arms anywhere. Somewhat relieved, I gave up my quest for a job and decided to simply stay at home and learn to be an even better dollar stretcher.

I had often dreamed of being a writer but shyness prevented me from really trying. Randal had often asked to see some of the things I had written, but I always refused. Finally, he was so insistent that I gave in. After reading them, he told me, "Mail them." After six months of hearing him say that, I finally gave in. Imagine my surprise when the first two manuscripts I mailed brought money to my mailbox. Within a year, I had sold manuscripts to seventeen different magazines.

Why am I telling you the story of my moneymaking endeavors? I think you have a right to know if I know what I'm talking about when I tell you it's possible to make money without leaving your home. I did it and you can, too. Running a home business is not always easy and it isn't always as profitable as you might wish, but compared with the alternative of leaving your home and children all day while you take an outside job, a home business seems much more attractive.

I decided to write these how-tos because I hope to be of help to other mothers who, like me, are full-time homemakers by choice, but who find it hard to live on a single paycheck. When

I was desperately longing for a way to stay at home with Karen, I wish someone could have come along to give me the answers to some of the problems I encountered. Even though I read every home career book in the library, I still felt shortchanged in the information I received. Most of them offered obvious facts or suggested jobs so exotic that they were unworkable in my situation.

I hope some of my experiences will help you and encourage you, too. I'll be praying that everyone who reads this book with the sincere intention of finding a home business in order to keep her career as a full-time homemaker will be successful.

Suggested Reading

Angel, Juvenal L. *Employment Opportunities for Men and Women After 60*. New York: World Trade Academy Press, Inc., 1969.

Boyd, Margaret A. *The Mail Order Crafts Catalogue*. Radnor, PA: Chilton Book Company, 1975.

Clark, Leta W. *How to Make Money with Your Crafts*. New York: William Morrow & Company, Inc., 1973.

Cooper, Joseph D. *A Woman's Guide to Part Time Jobs*. Garden City: Doubleday & Company, Inc. Dolphin Books, 1963.

Feinman, Jeffrey. *100 Sure Fire Businesses You Can Start with Little or No Investment*. Chicago: Playboy Press, 1976.

Gibson, Mary Bass. *The Family Circle Book of Careers at Home*. Chicago: Cowles Book Company, Inc., 1971.

Hewitt, Geof. *How to Be Successfully Self-employed Working for Yourself*. Emmaus, PA: Rodale Press, 1977.

Hoffman, Ray. *Extra Dollars Easy Money-making Ideas for Retired People*. New York: Stein and Day Publishers, 1977.

Lapin, Lynne and Wones, Betsy, eds. *1978 Art and Crafts Market*. Cincinnati: Writer's Digest Books, 1977.

J. K. Lasser Tax Institute. *J. K. Lasser's How to Run a Small Business*. New York: McGraw-Hill Book Company, 4th edn., 1974.

LeBlanc, Jerry. *The Moonlighter's Manual, 300 Ways to Make Money in Your Spare Time*. Los Angeles: Nash Publishing Corporation, 1969.

The Mother Earth News, The Mother Earth News Handbook of Home Business Ideas and Plans. New York: Bantam Books, 1976.

Robertson, Laura. *How to Start a Money-making Business at Home*. New York: Frederick Fell, Inc., 1969.

Scott, Michael. *The Crafts Business Encyclopedia*. New York: Harcourt, Brace, Jovanovich, 1977.

Sommer, Elyse. *Career Opportunities in Crafts*. New York: Crown Publishers, Inc., 1977.

Stern, Alfred. *How Mail Order Fortunes Are Made*. New York: Arco Publishing Co., Inc., 1970.

Szykitka, Walter. *How to Be Your Own Boss*. New York: New American Library, 1978.

Weaver, Peter. *You, Inc.* Garden City: Doubleday & Company, Inc., 1973.

Wettlaufer, George and Nancy. *The Craftsman's Survival Manual, Making a Full or Part Time Living from Your Craft*. Englewood Cliffs, NJ: Prentice-Hall, Inc., 1974.

Wood, Jane. *Selling What You Make*. Baltimore: Penguin Books, Inc., 1973.

MAGAZINES

Arts and Crafts

American Artist Business Letter
2160 Patterson Street
Cincinnati, OH 45214

Craft Horizons
A Publication of the American Crafts Council
44 West 53rd Street
New York, NY 10019

Photo Artist, USA
Sun Country Enterprises, Inc.
501–503 North Virginia Avenue
Winter Park, FL 32789

Sunshine Artists
Sun Country Enterprises, Inc.
501–503 N. Virginia Avenue
Winter Park, FL 32789

Handicrafts That Sell
Tower Press
P.O. Box 428
Seabrook, NH 03874

The Goodfellow Newsletter
P.O. Box 4520
Berkeley, CA 94704

Business Ideas and How-To

Free Enterprise
1212 Avenue of the Americas
New York, NY 10036

The Mother Earth News
P.O. Box 70
Hendersonville, NC 28739
(This publication also sells back issues and books on helpful subjects.)

Mail Order

Direct Marketing
224 Seventh Street
Garden City, NY 11530
(This publication also sells back issues and reprints of articles. Ask for the Index to New Ideas and Methods to Choose from for Your Campaign.)

INFORMATION SOURCES

U.S. Industrial Directory
Cahners Publishing Company
89 Franklin Street
Boston, MA 02110

Thomas' Register of American Manufacturers
Thomas Publishing Company
One Penn Plaza
New York, NY 10001

International Yellow Pages
The Reuben H. Donnelley Corporation
235 East 45th Street
New York, NY 10017

Direct Mail List Rates and Data
Standard Rate and Data Service, Inc.
5201 Old Orchard Road
Skokie, IL 60077

Dun and Bradstreet Reference

GOVERNMENT PUBLICATIONS

"An Information Aid For Inventors"
Department of Commerce
14th Street
Washington, DC 20231

"General Information Concerning Patents"
Department of Commerce
14th Street
Washington, DC 20231

"General Information On Copyrights"
Library of Congress
First Street
Washington, DC 20540

"Tax Guide For Small Businesses"
U.S. Government Printing Office
Washington, DC 20401

"Your Federal Income Tax"
U.S. Government Printing Office
Washington, DC 20401

"U.S. Postal Service Mailer's Guide"
available at local post offices

"Craft Resources"
by Gerald E. Ely
Economics, Statistics, and Cooperative Service
Room 550 GHI
U.S. Department of Agriculture
Washington, DC 20250

"Cooperative Approach to Crafts"
by Gerald E. Ely
Economics, Statistics, and Cooperative Service
Room 550 GHI
U.S. Department of Agriculture
Washington, DC 20250

SMALL BUSINESS ADMINISTRATION

The following leaflets are available from the SBA:

Small Business Administration
P.O. Box 15434
Fort Worth, TX 76119

To order, write first to determine which titles are available as titles change from time to time. Up to twenty titles of leaflets may be ordered free of charge. Additional in-depth booklets are also available for a small fee. Request a complete list of titles.

The ABC's of Borrowing
Association Services for Small Businesses
Basic Library Reference Sources
Financial Management
Getting the Facts for Income Tax Reporting
Handicrafts
Home Businesses
Incorporating a Small Business
Insurance Checklist for Small Business
Marketing Research Procedures
National Mailing List Houses
Plan Your Advertising Budget
Problems in Managing a Family-owned Business
Public Relations for Small Business
Selling by Mail Order
Selling Products on Consignment
Signs and Your Business
Steps in Meeting Your Tax Obligations
What Is the Best Selling Price?